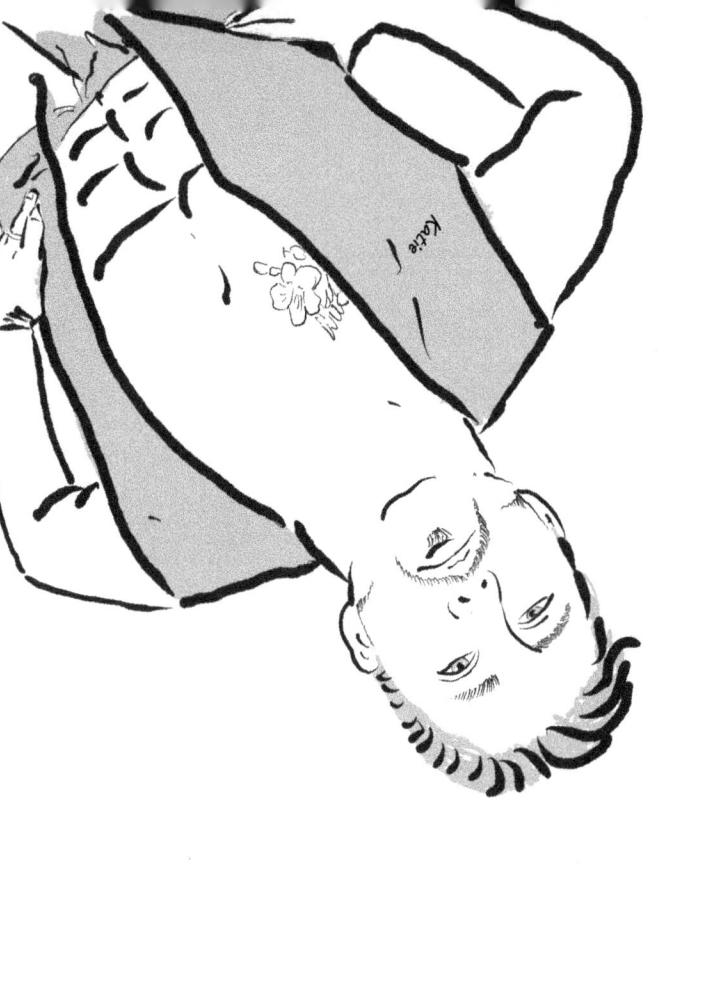
Katie

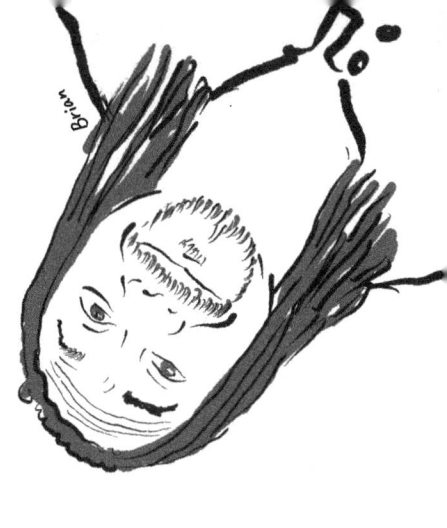
Brian

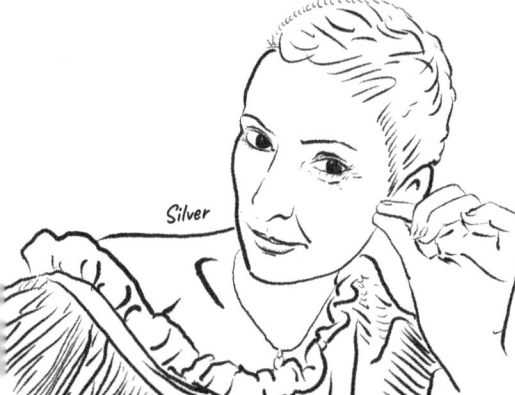
Silver

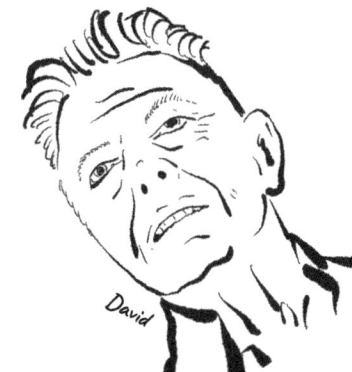
David

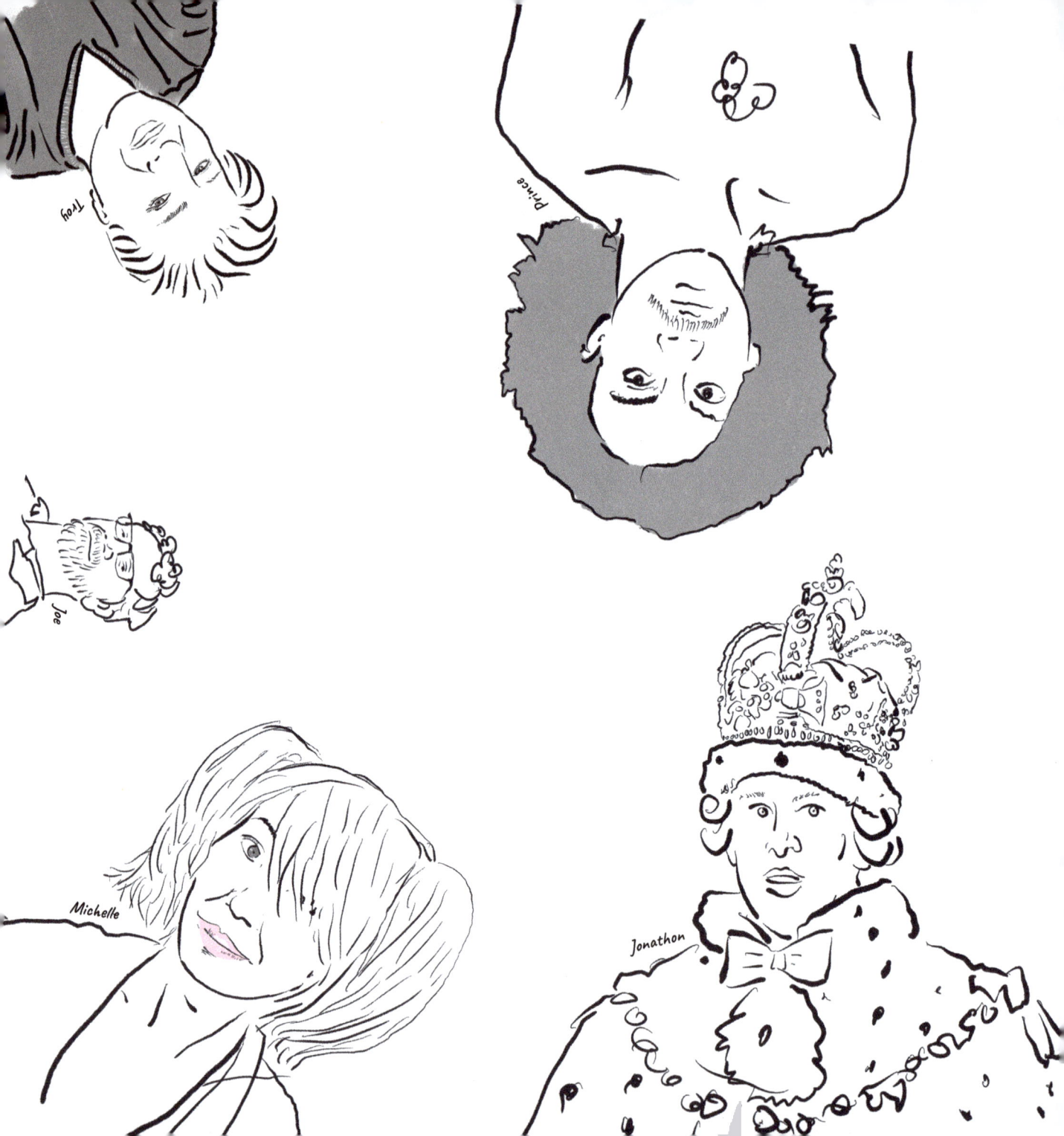

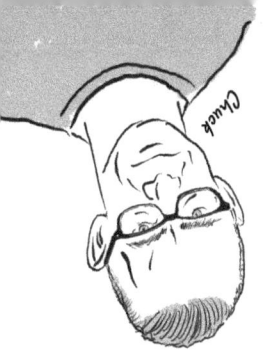

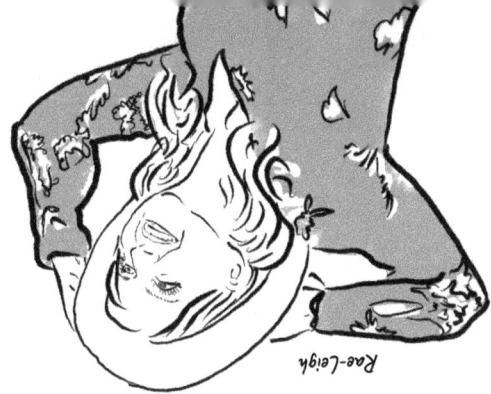

dancing,
and other
problems

A Very 2020 Sketchbook

(Feel free to Banksy this book up)

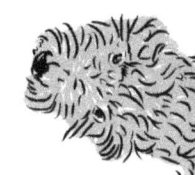

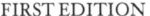

FIRST EDITION

This is a work of fiction and satire. A good chunk of my sanity plan during this Covid time has been drawing. Friends, notable artists/influences, and people I follow on Social media. In a time we are all so apart, it has been incredibly cathartic. It started as a book about User Experience Design, but turned out to be an Art Book centered in Human Centered Design. Quit your job. Start a fight. Prove you're alive. If you don't claim your humanity you will become a statistic. You have been warned.....Tyler. All rights reserved. No part of this book may be reproduced or used in any manner without written permission of the copyright owner except for the use of quotations in a book review.

Copyright © 2021 by Norville Parchment

Find me @norvilleparchment

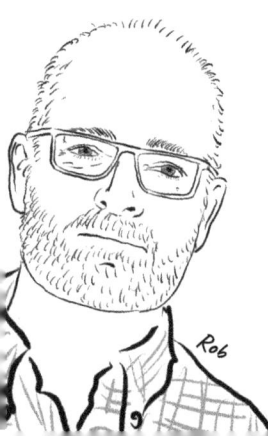

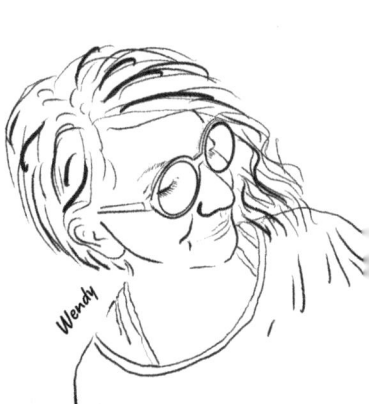

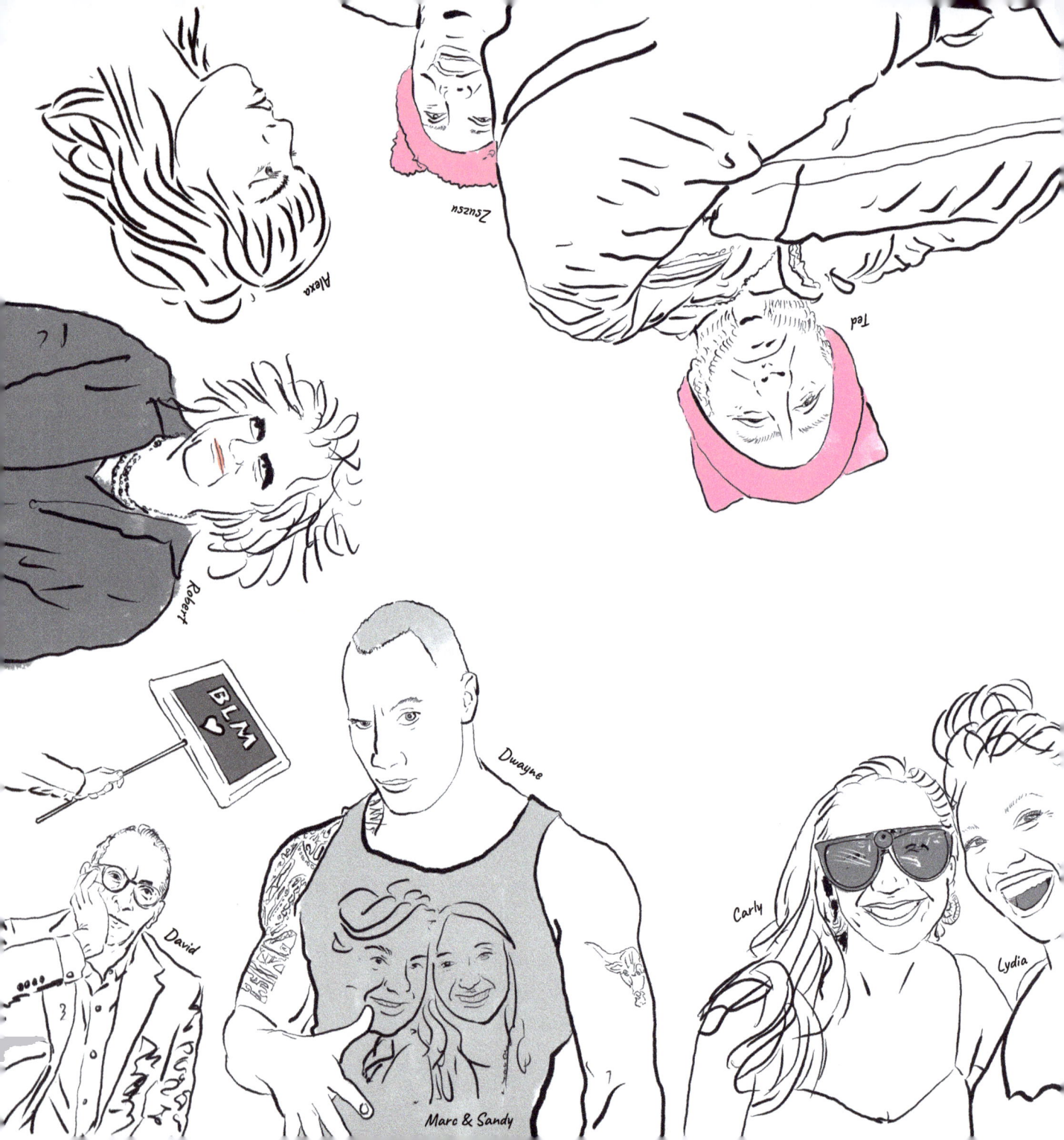

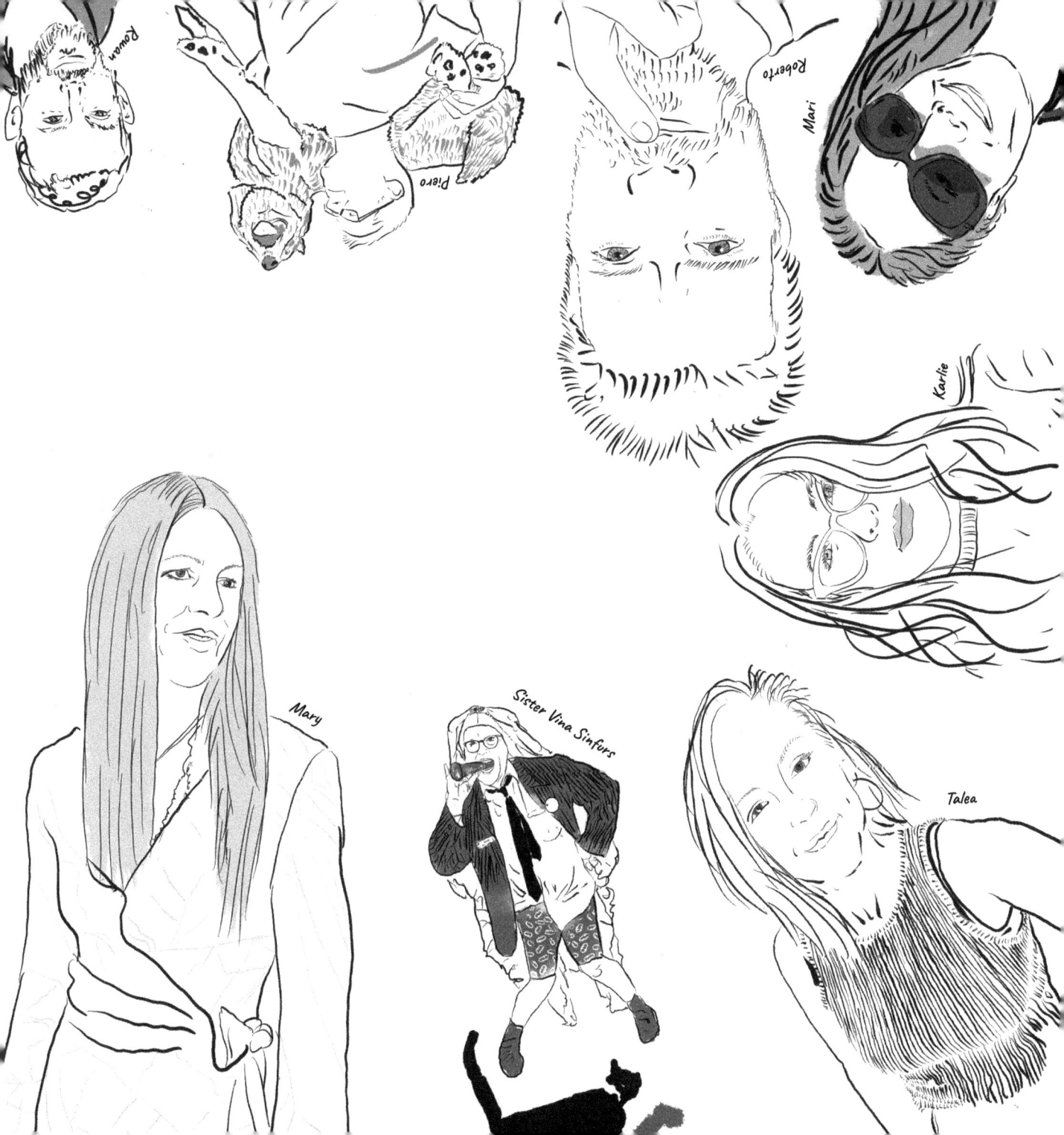

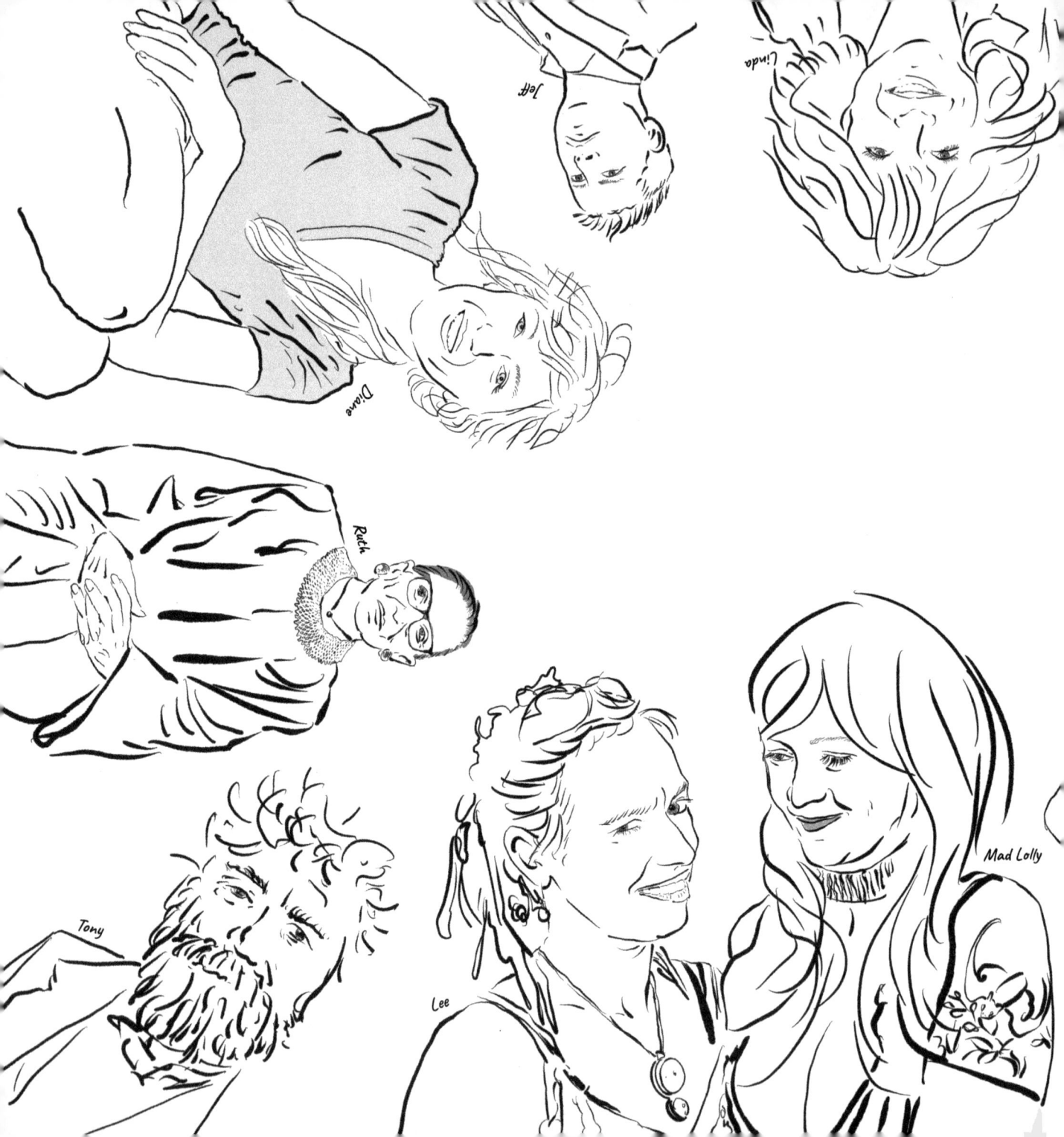

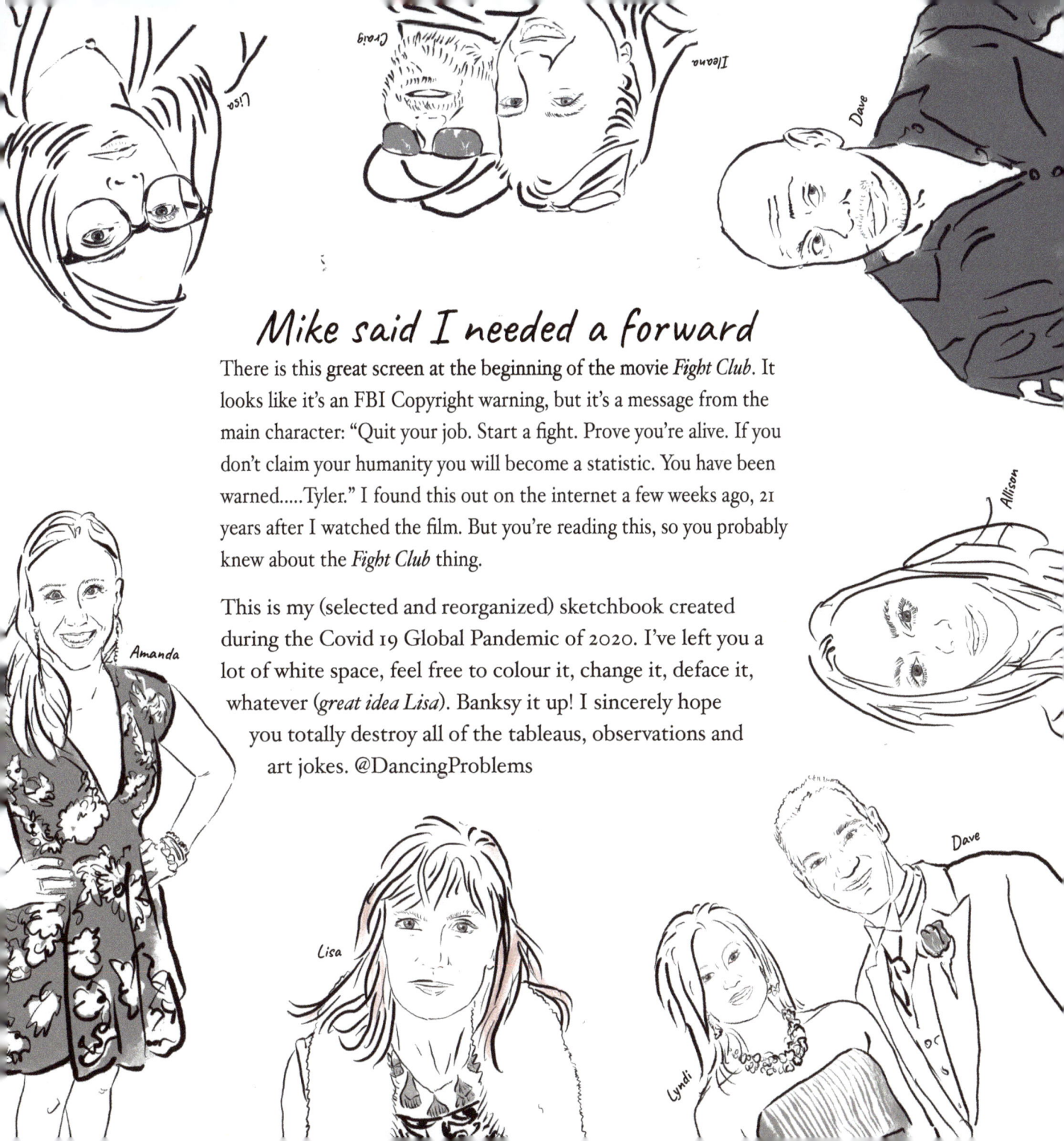

Mike said I needed a forward

There is this great screen at the beginning of the movie *Fight Club*. It looks like it's an FBI Copyright warning, but it's a message from the main character: "Quit your job. Start a fight. Prove you're alive. If you don't claim your humanity you will become a statistic. You have been warned.....Tyler." I found this out on the internet a few weeks ago, 21 years after I watched the film. But you're reading this, so you probably knew about the *Fight Club* thing.

This is my (selected and reorganized) sketchbook created during the Covid 19 Global Pandemic of 2020. I've left you a lot of white space, feel free to colour it, change it, deface it, whatever (*great idea Lisa*). Banksy it up! I sincerely hope you totally destroy all of the tableaus, observations and art jokes. @DancingProblems

Lisa

Craig

Ileana

Dave

Allison

Amanda

Lisa

Lyndi

Dave

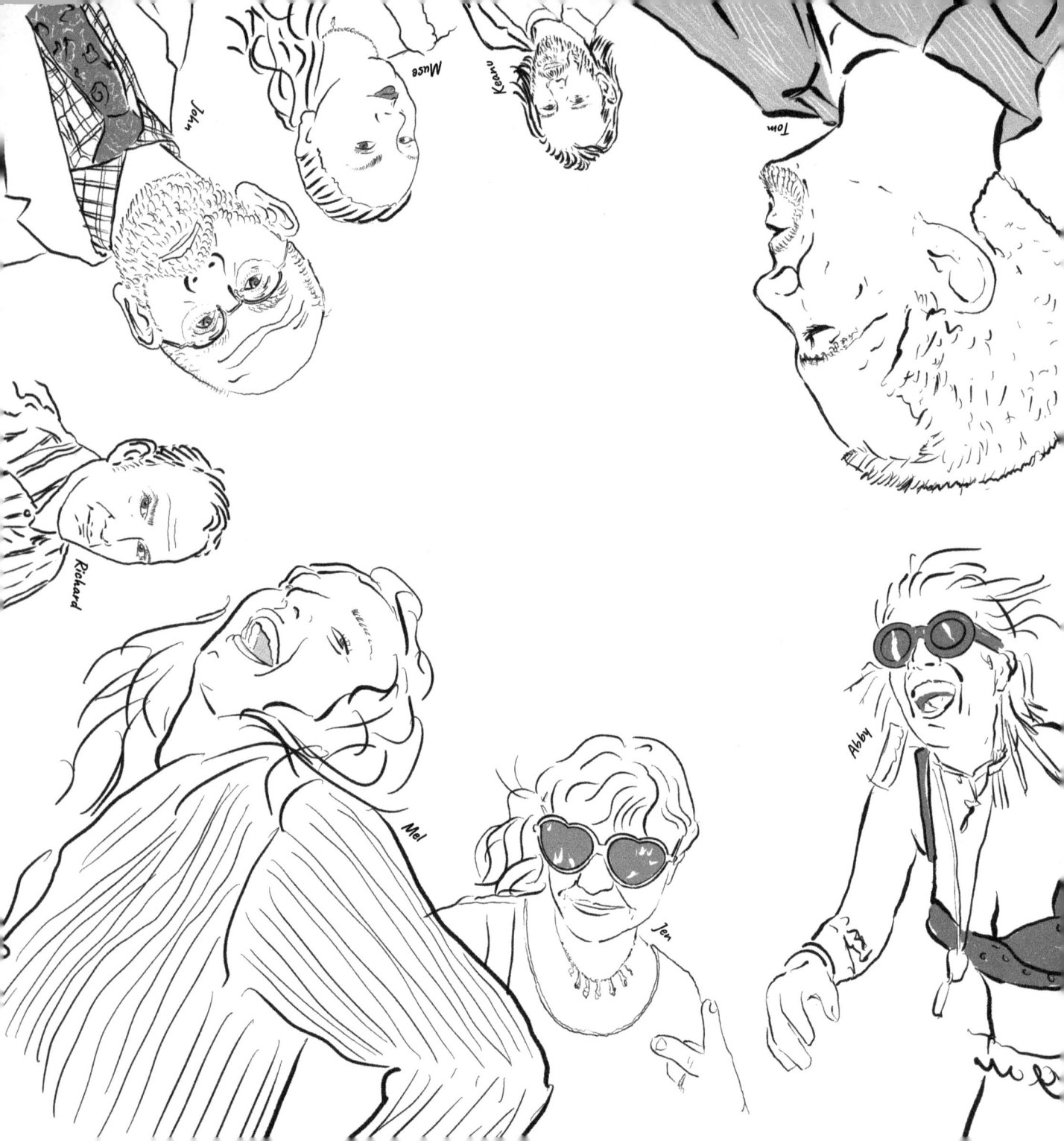

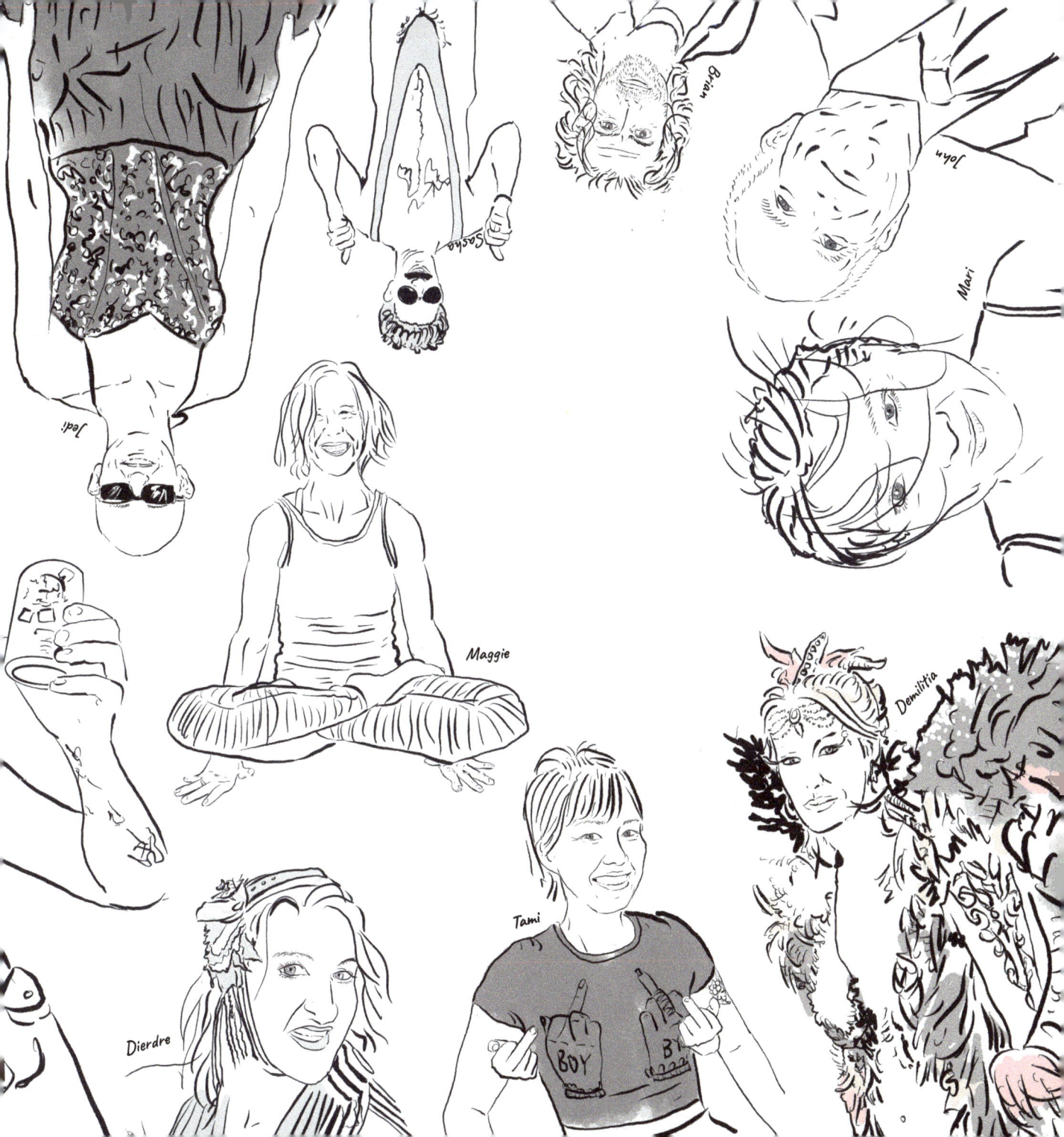

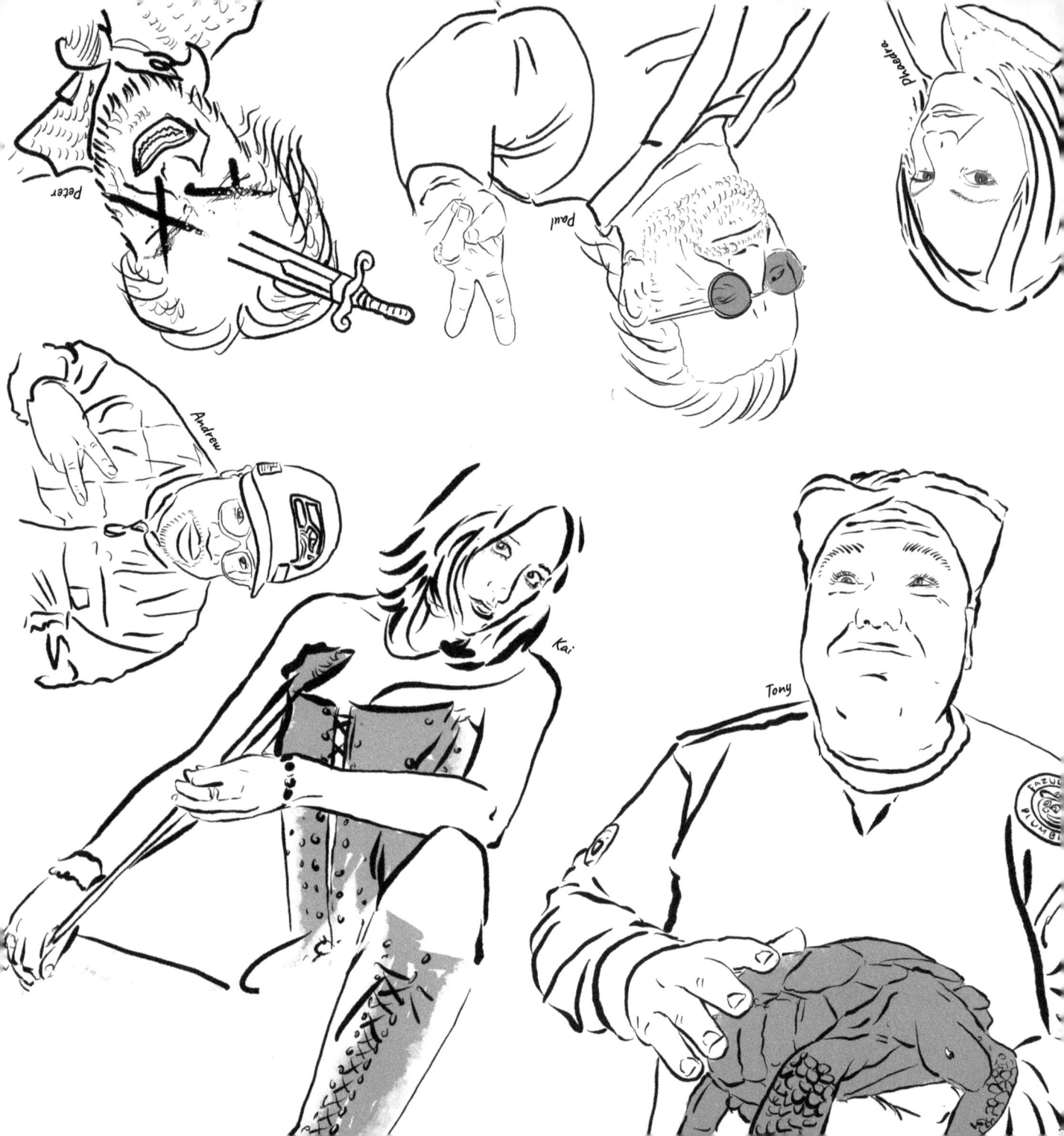

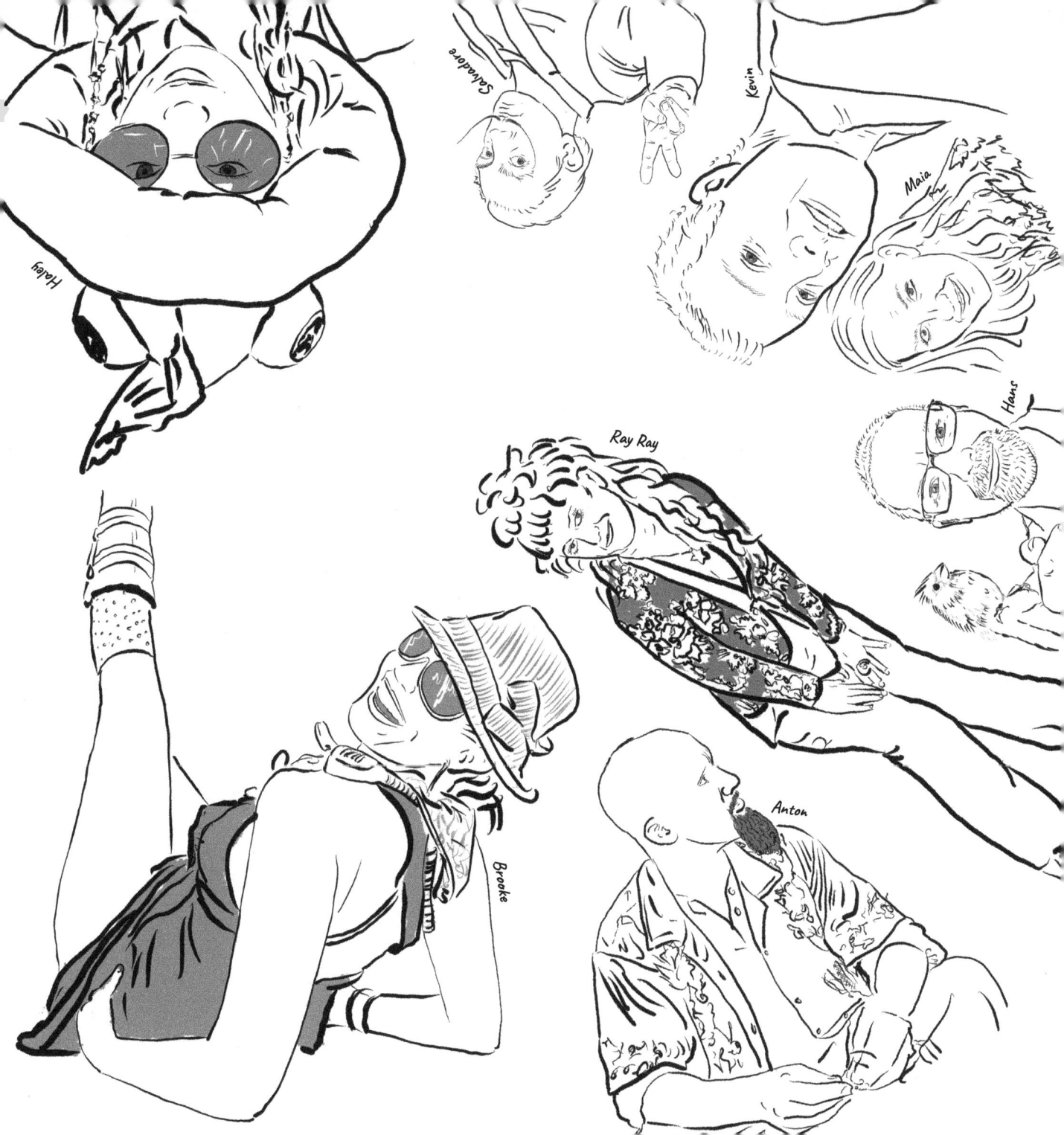

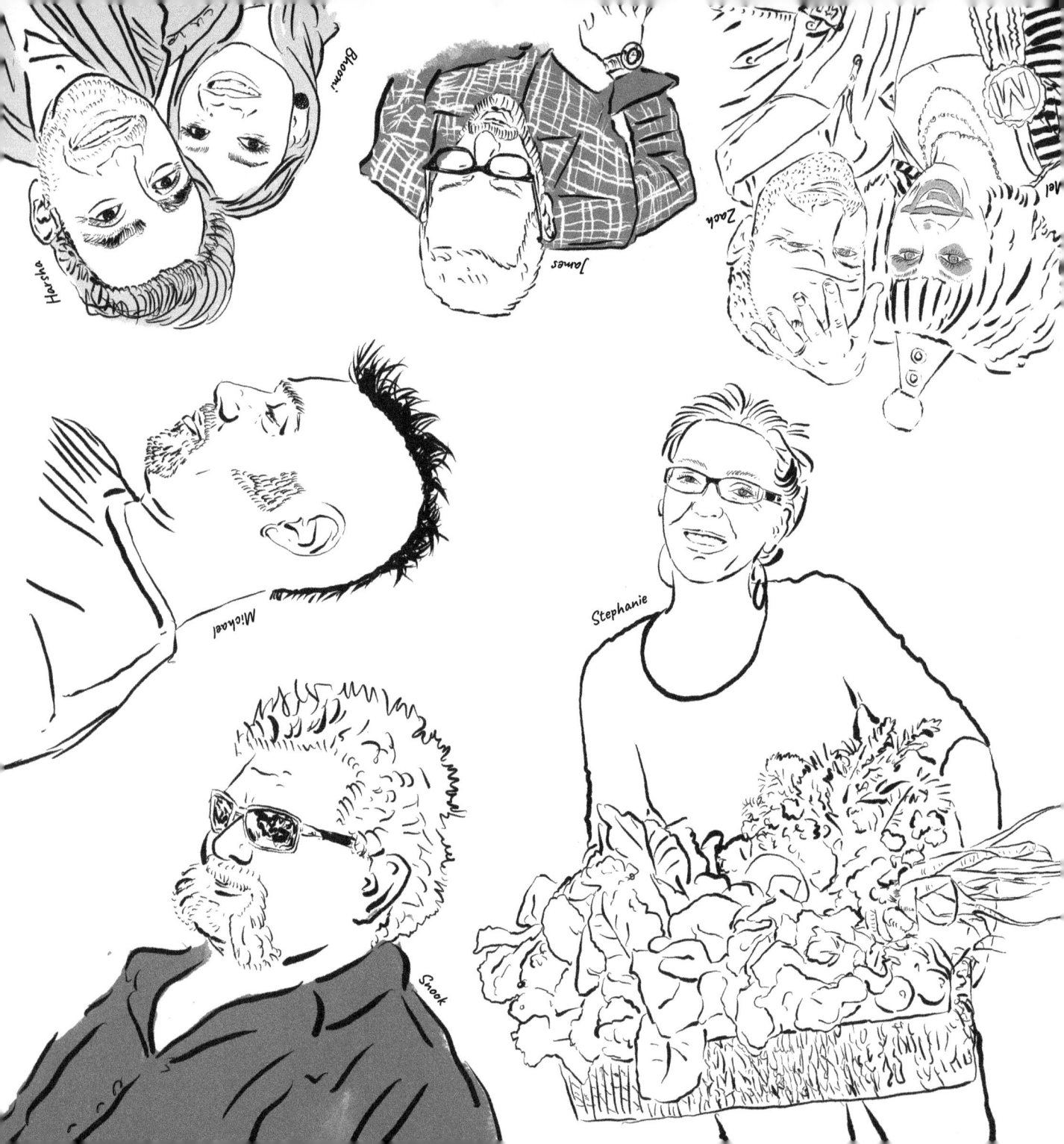

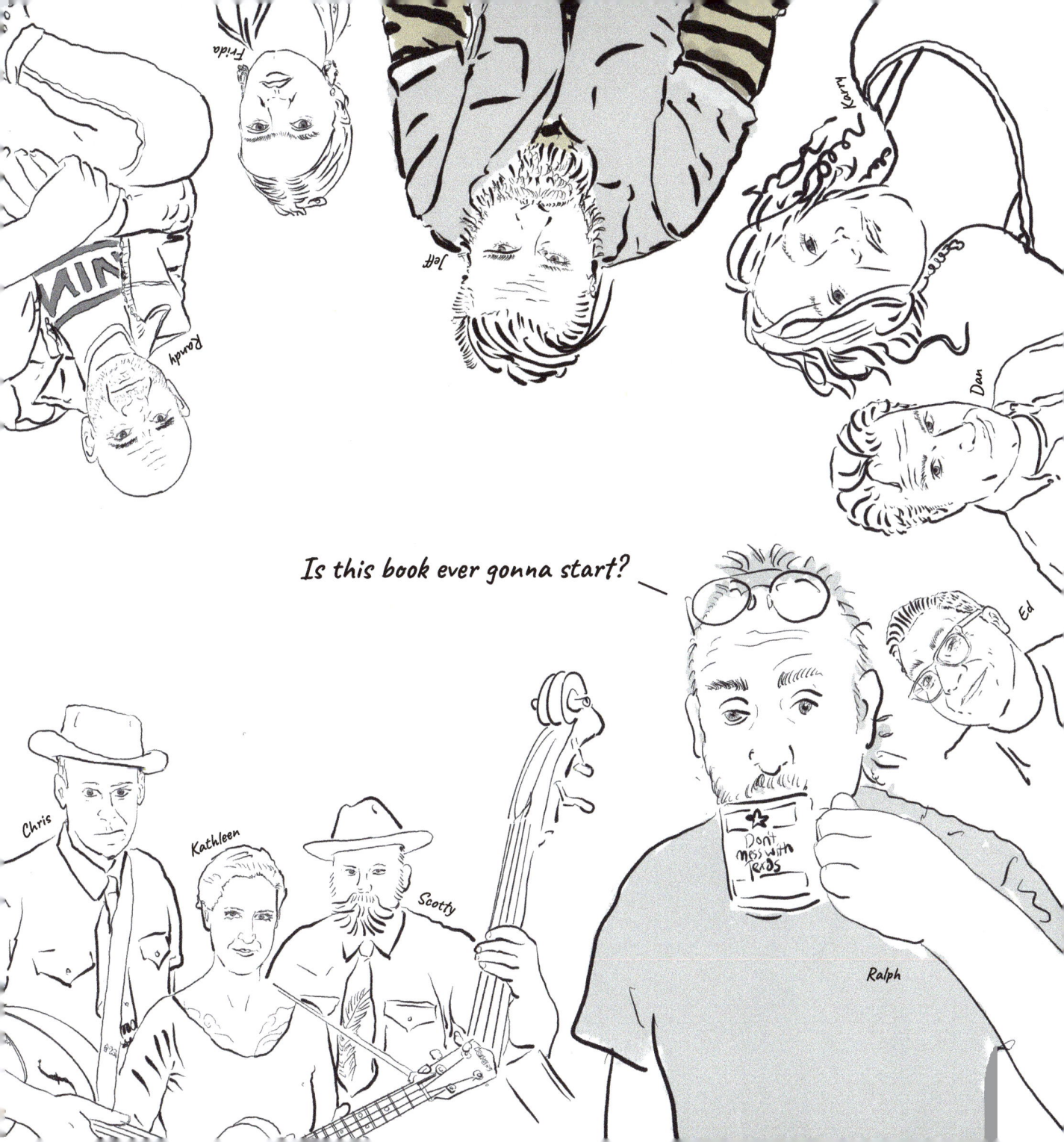

Is this book ever gonna start?

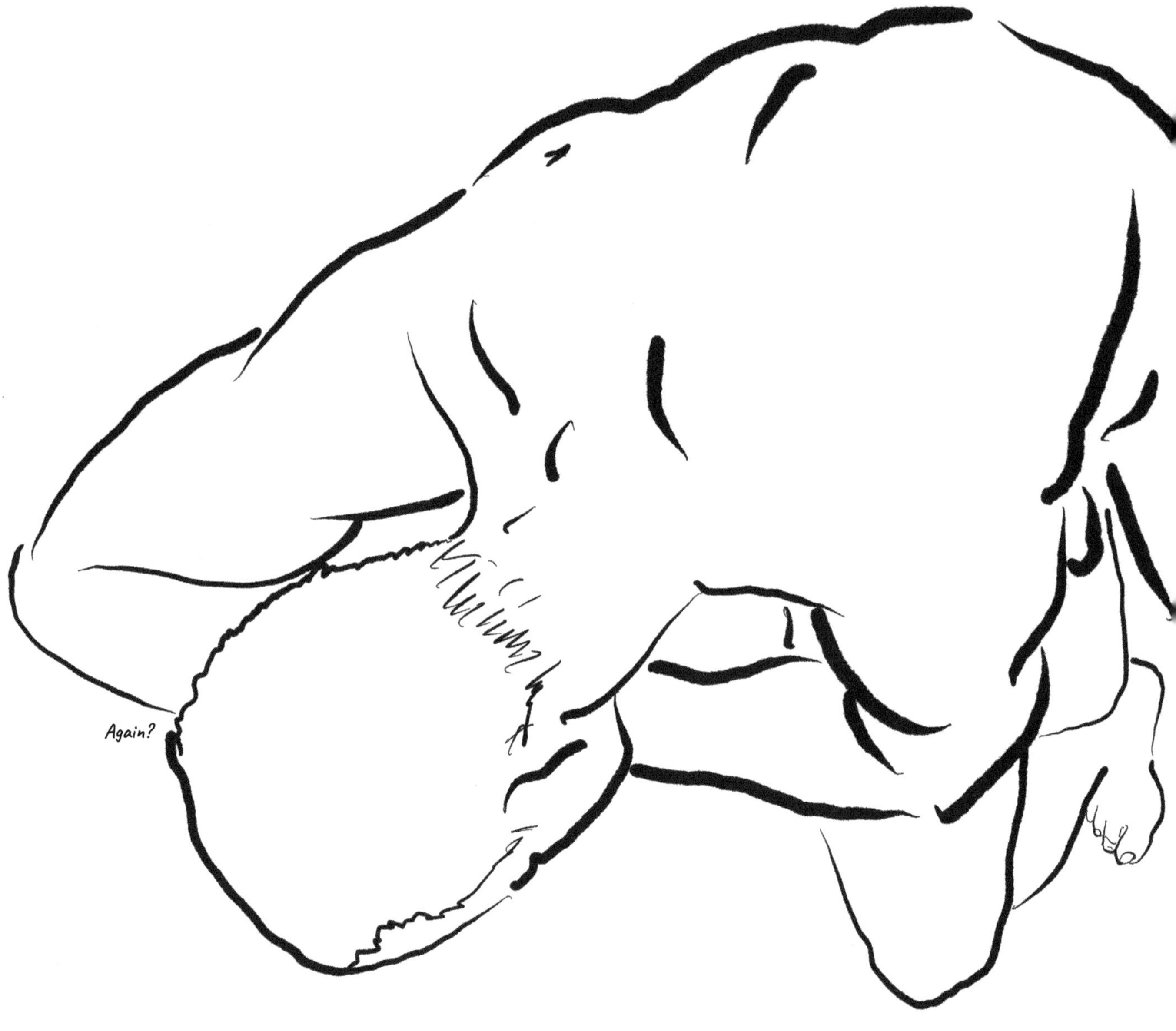

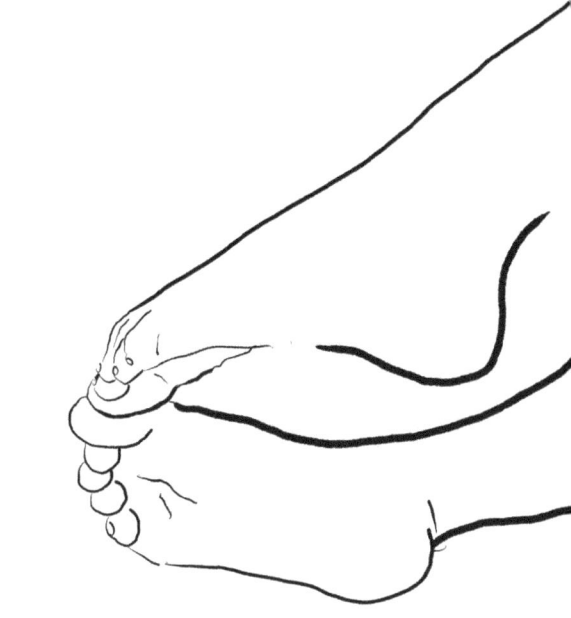

Monday(s)

Celebrity Sayings

Politics

An Elegant Rendition of the Spins

A Final Thought

Appendix

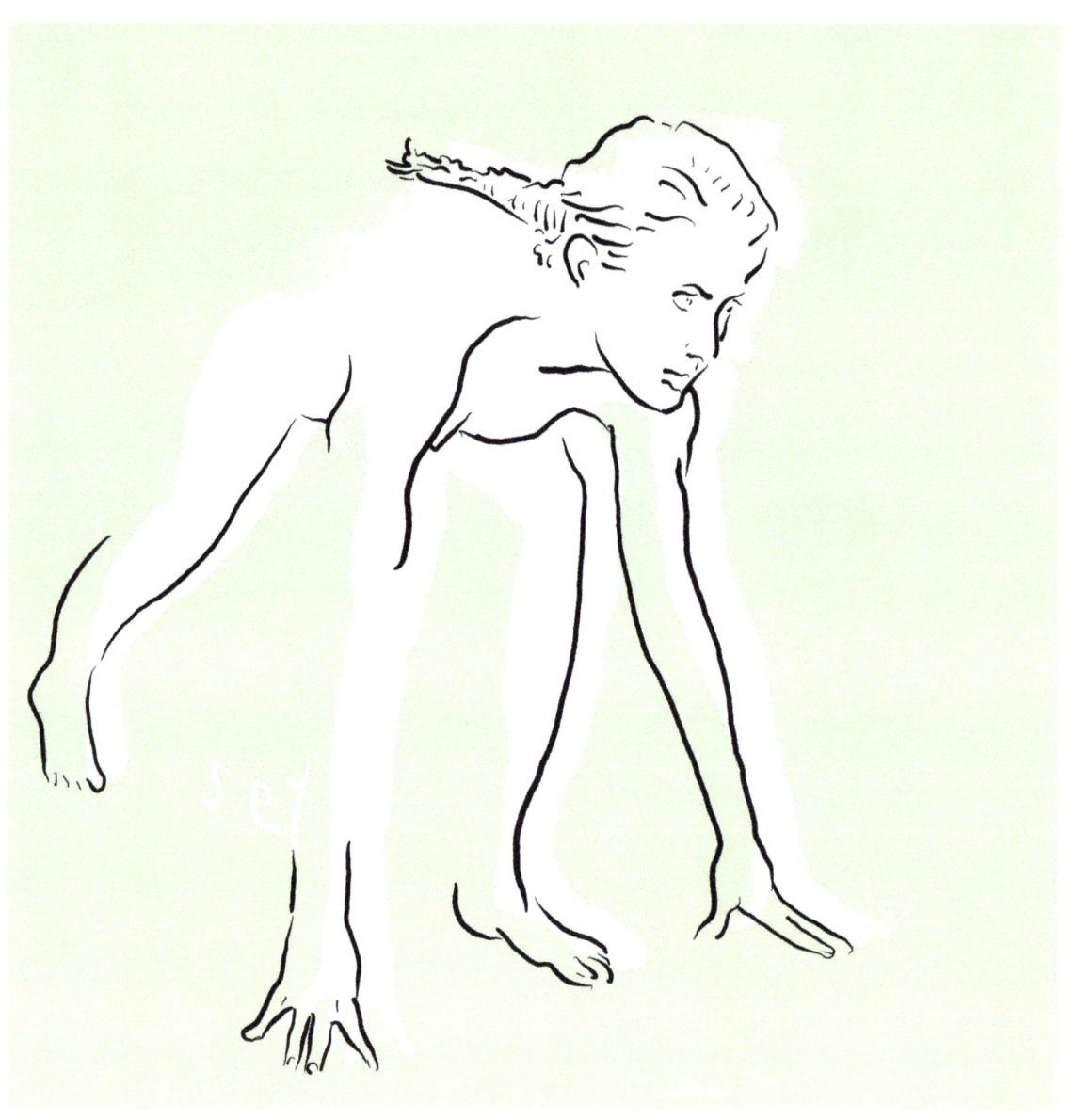

Chapter One

Monday(s)

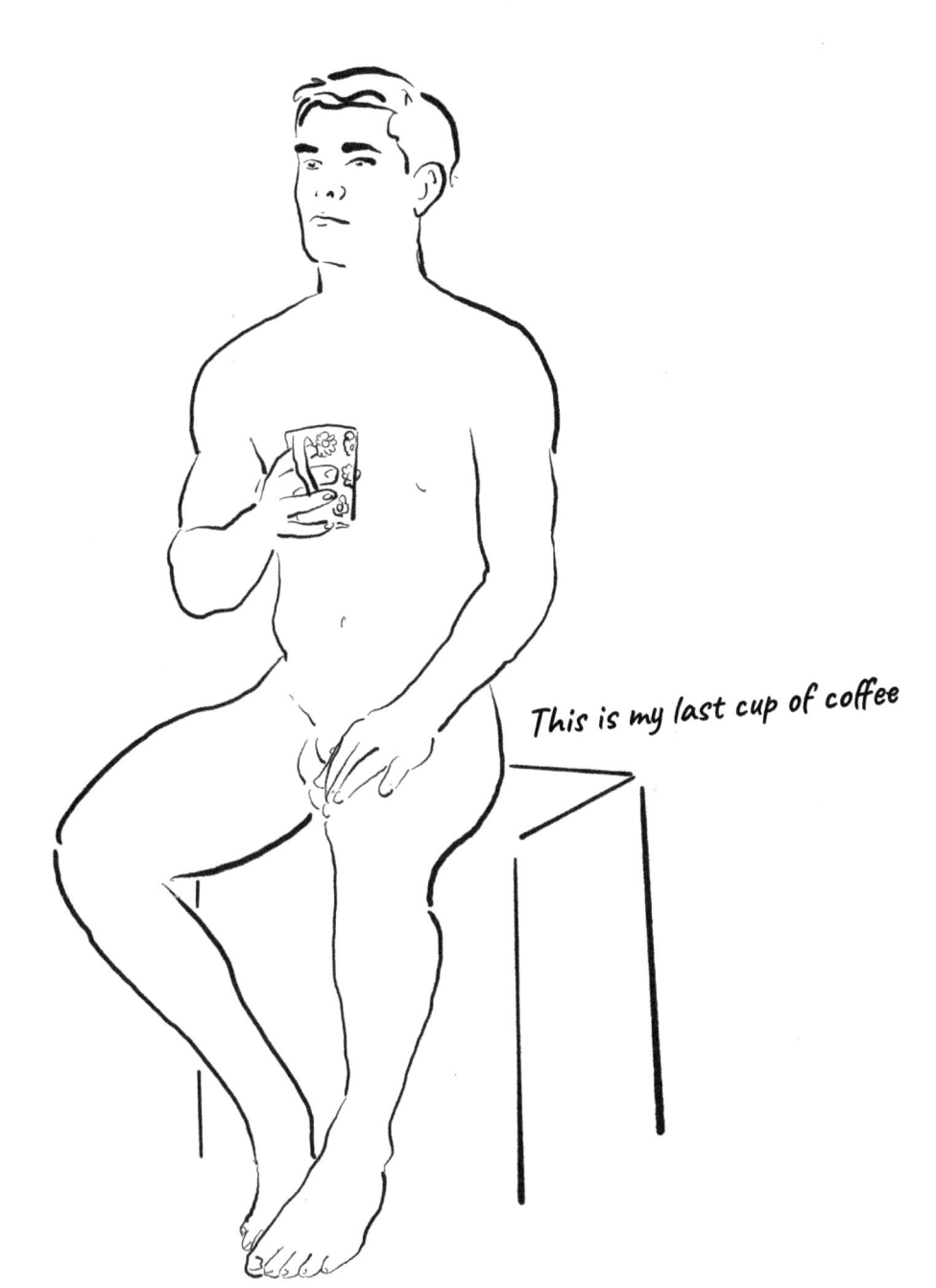

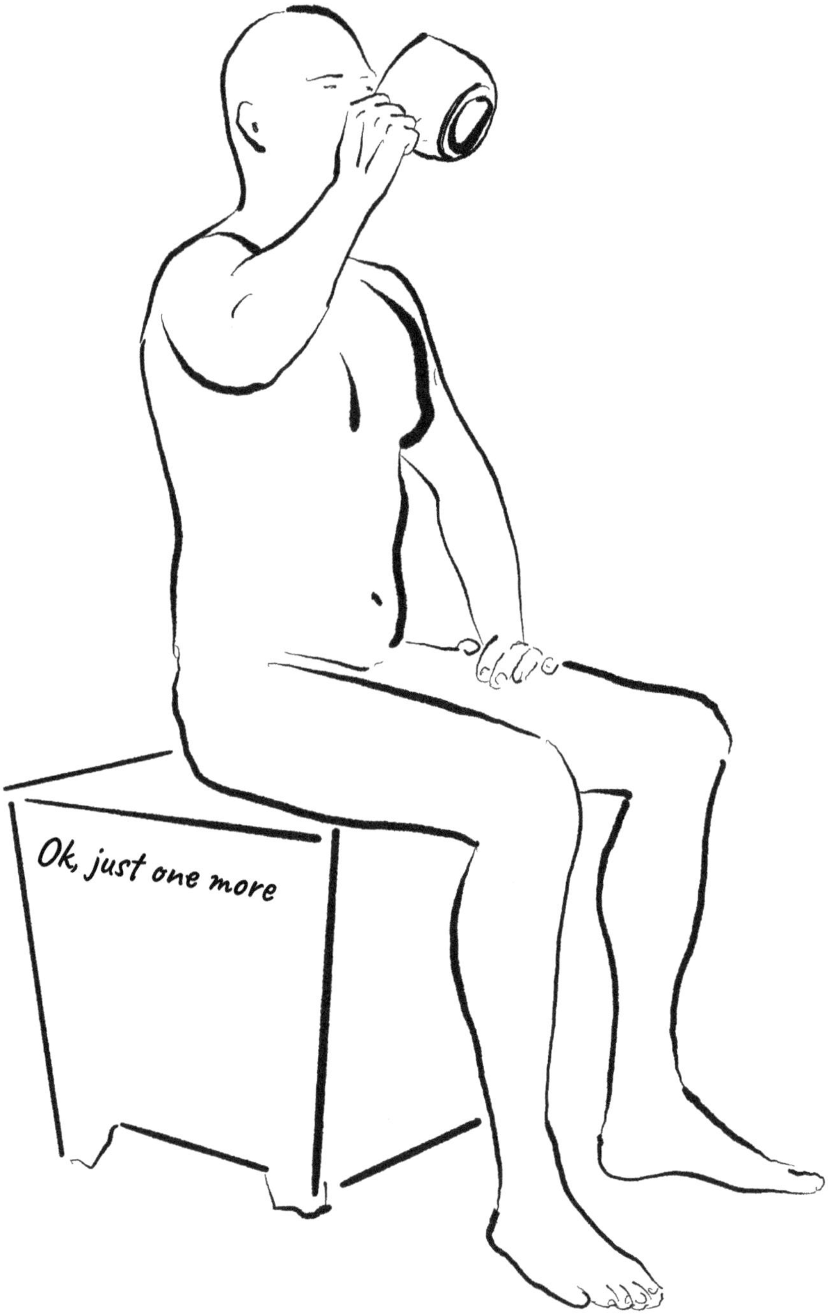

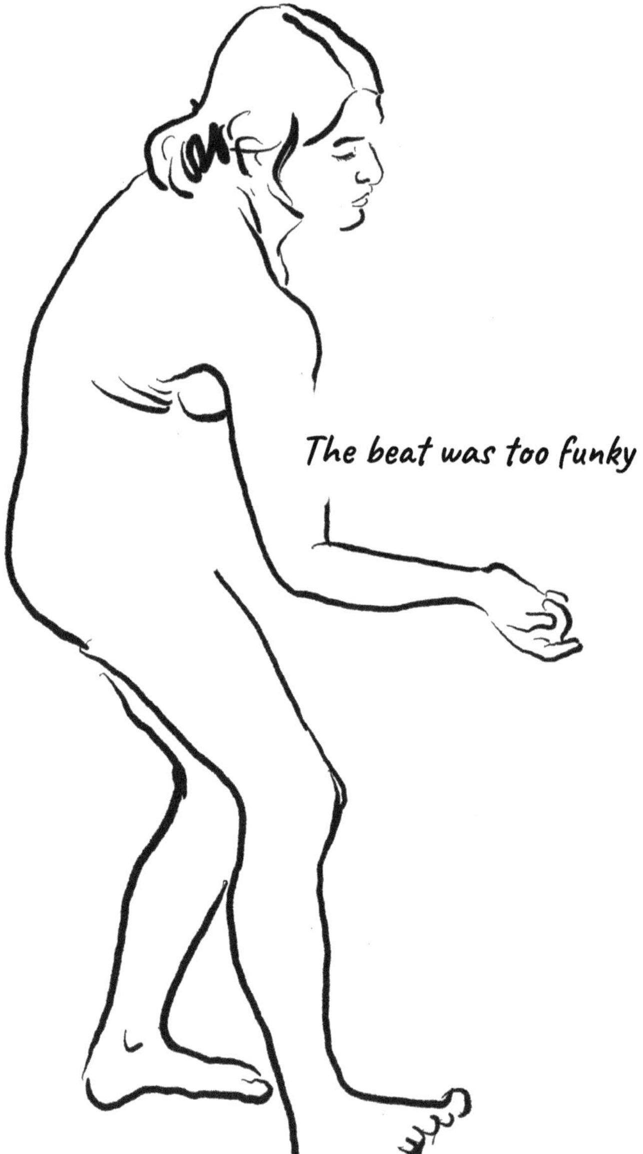

The beat was too funky

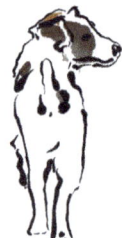 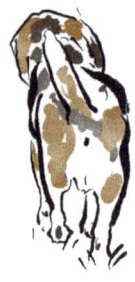

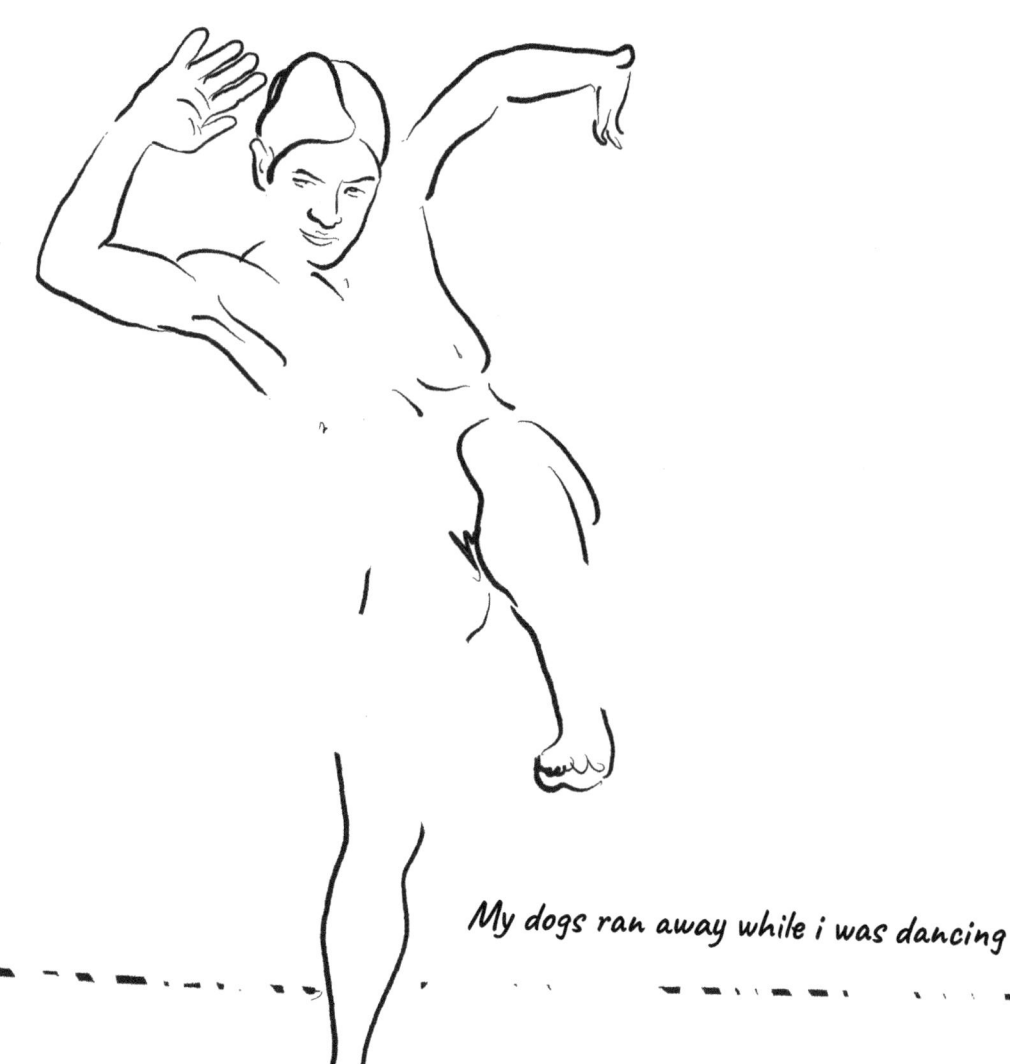

My dogs ran away while i was dancing

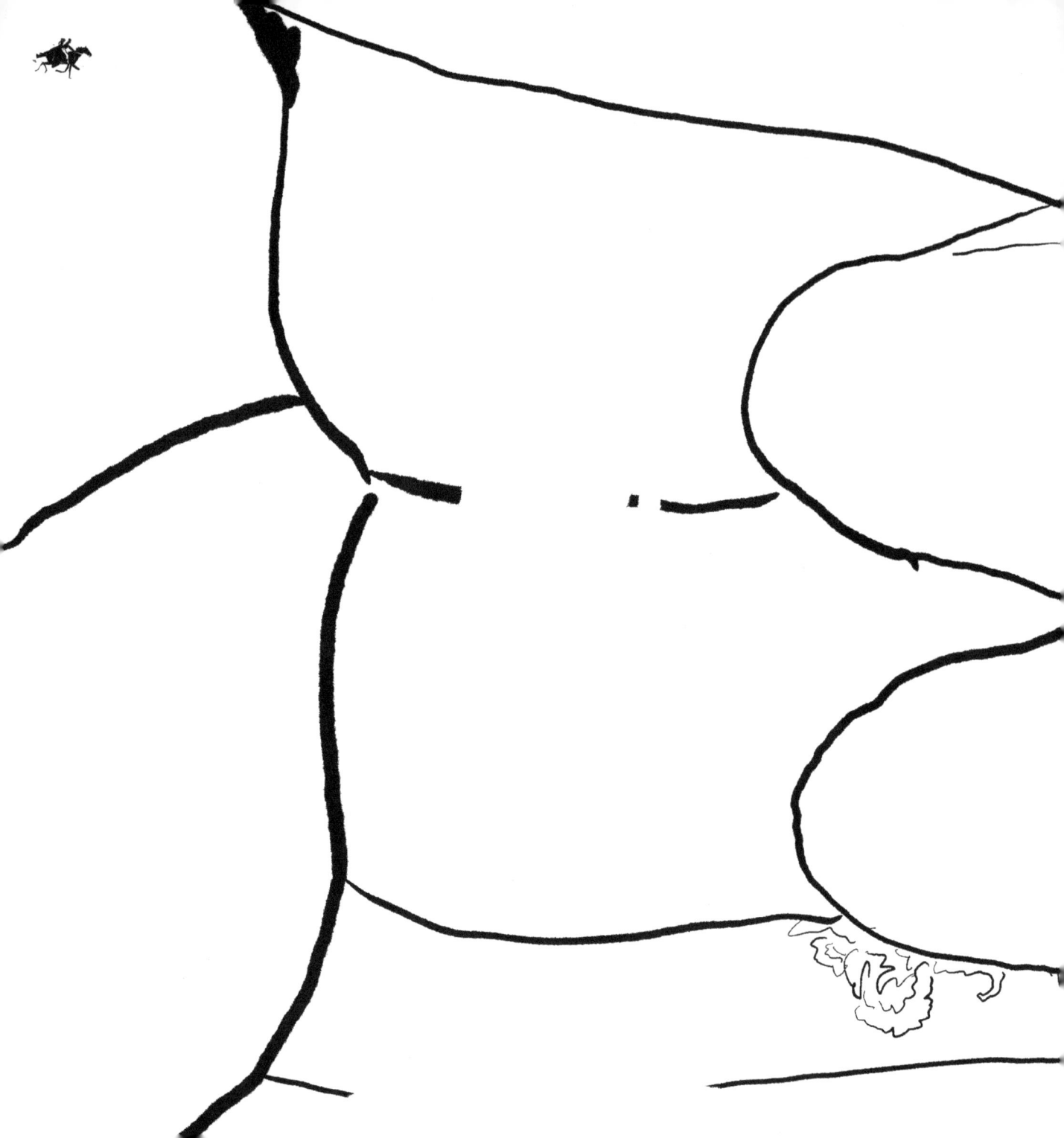

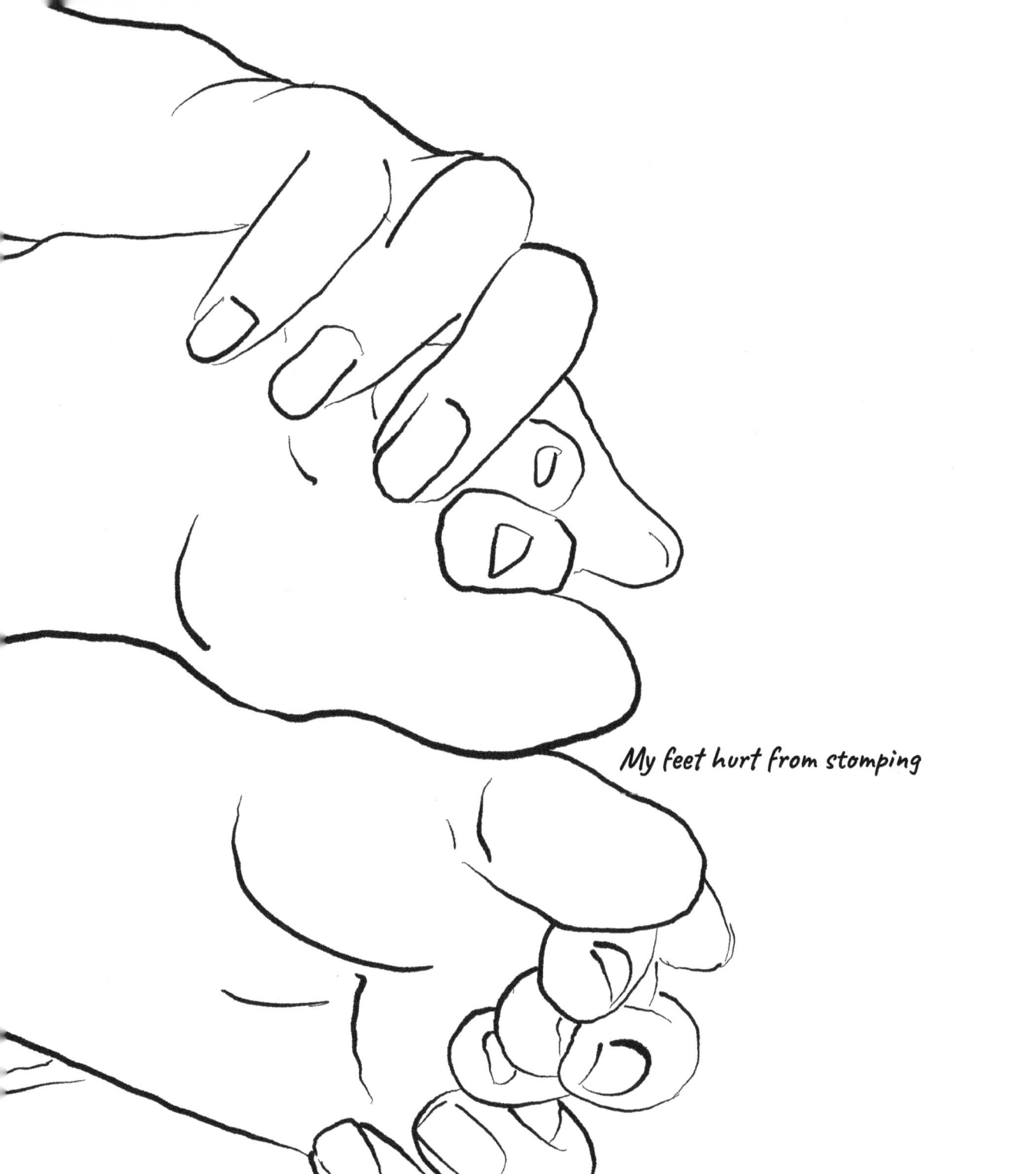

My feet hurt from stomping

this bitch

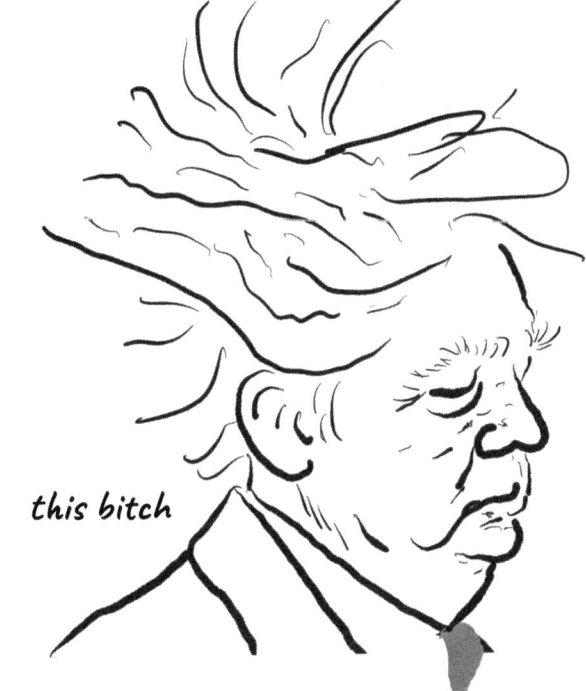

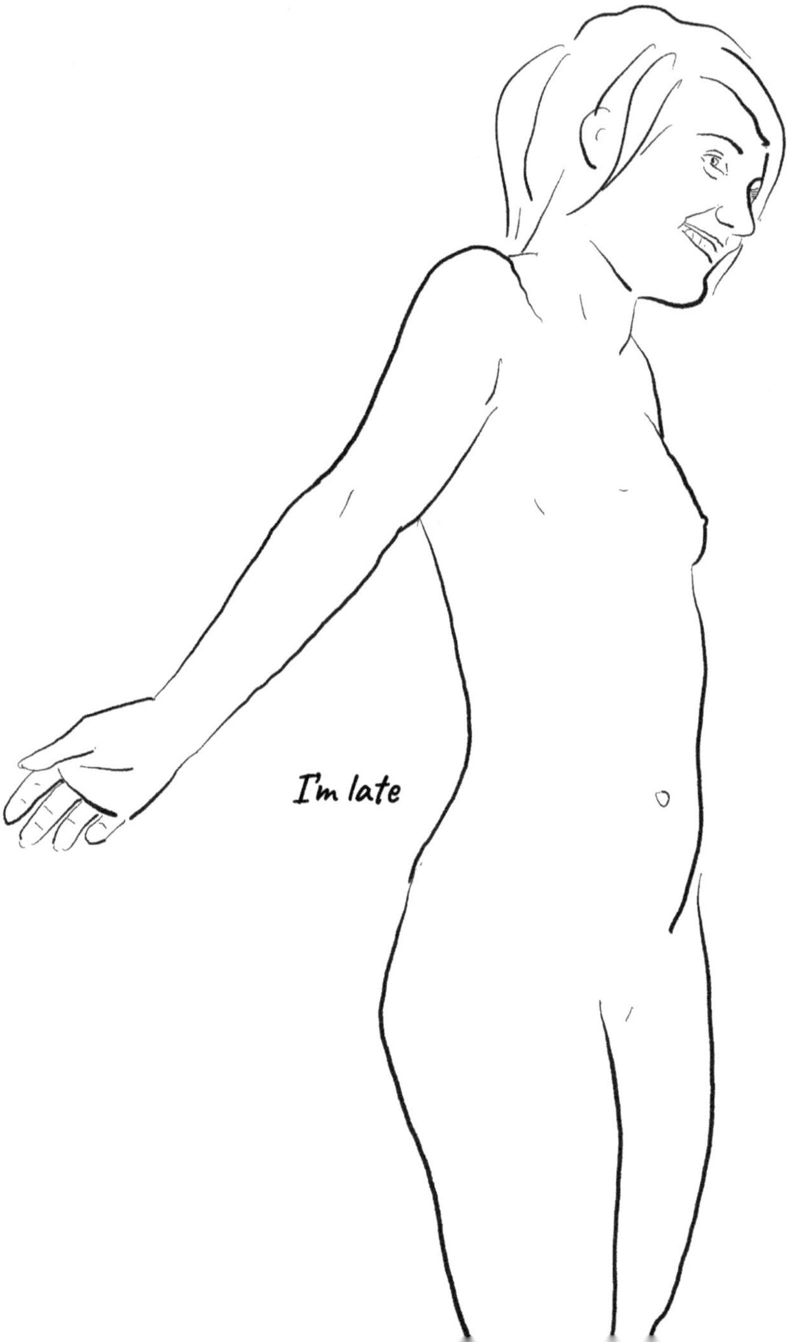

I'm late

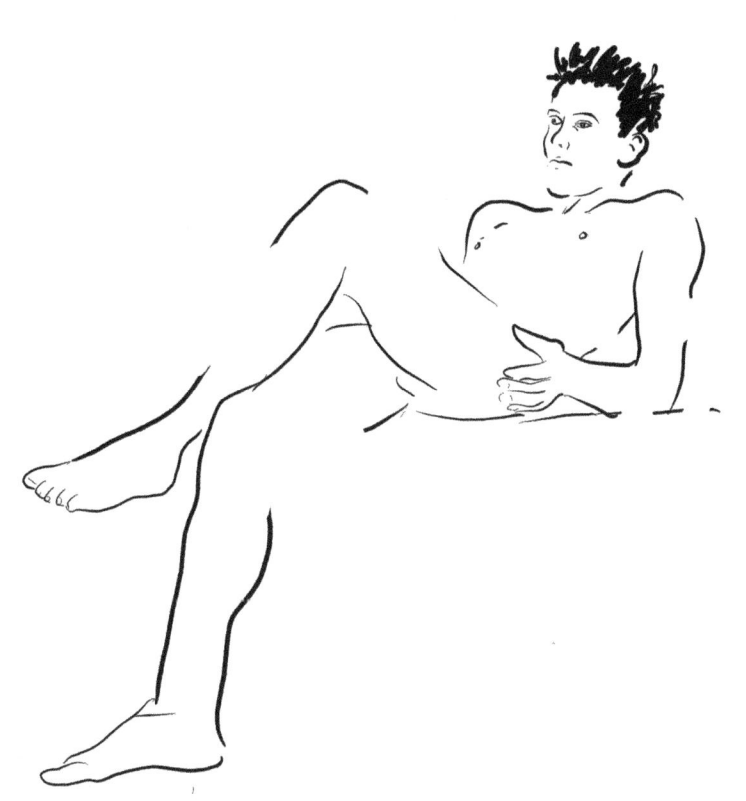

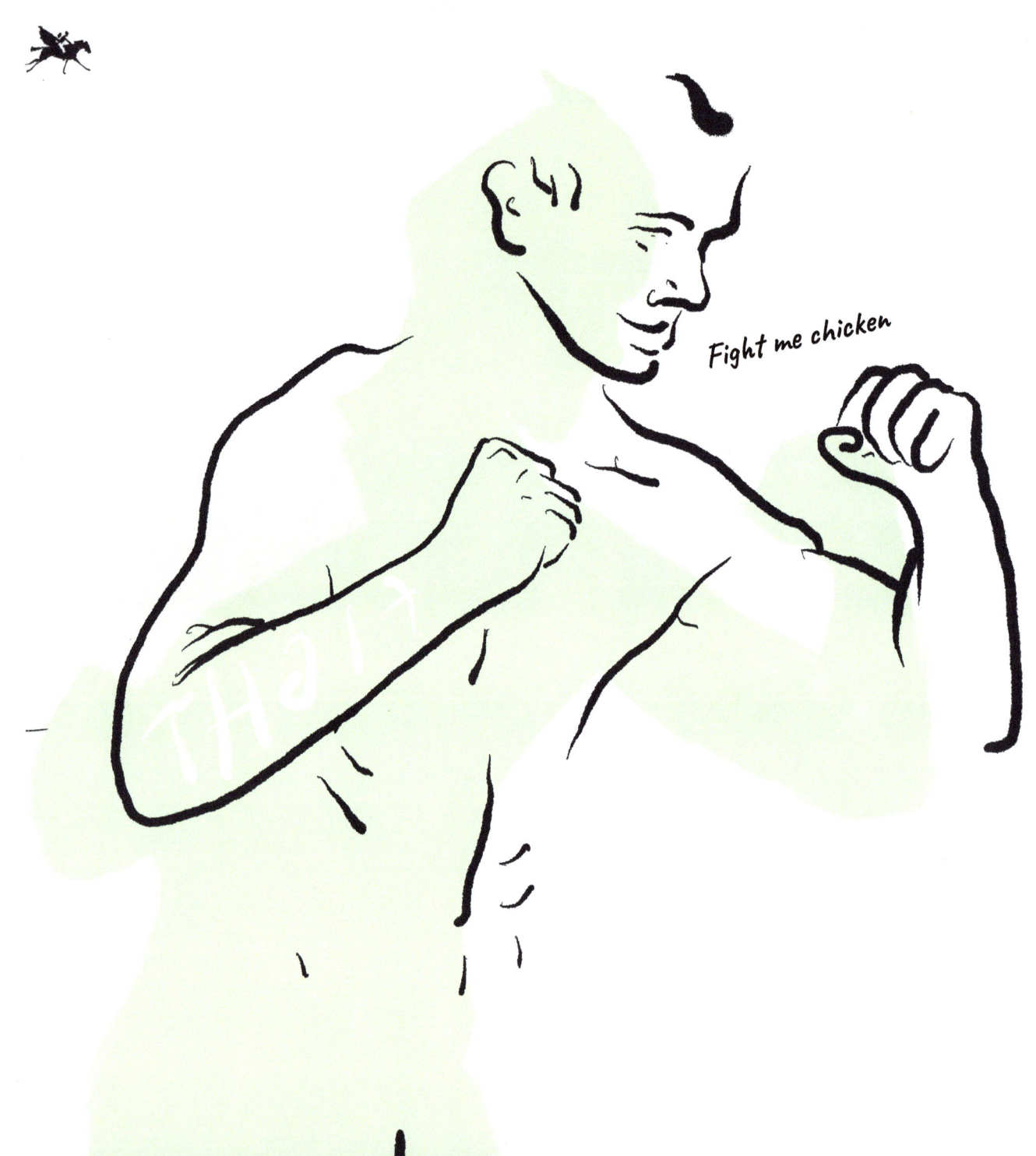

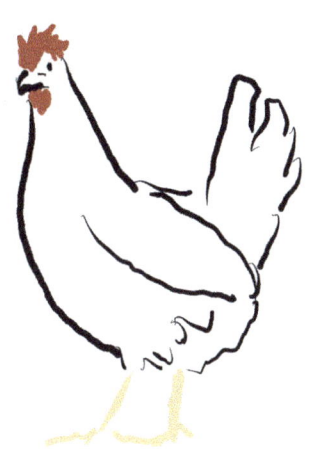

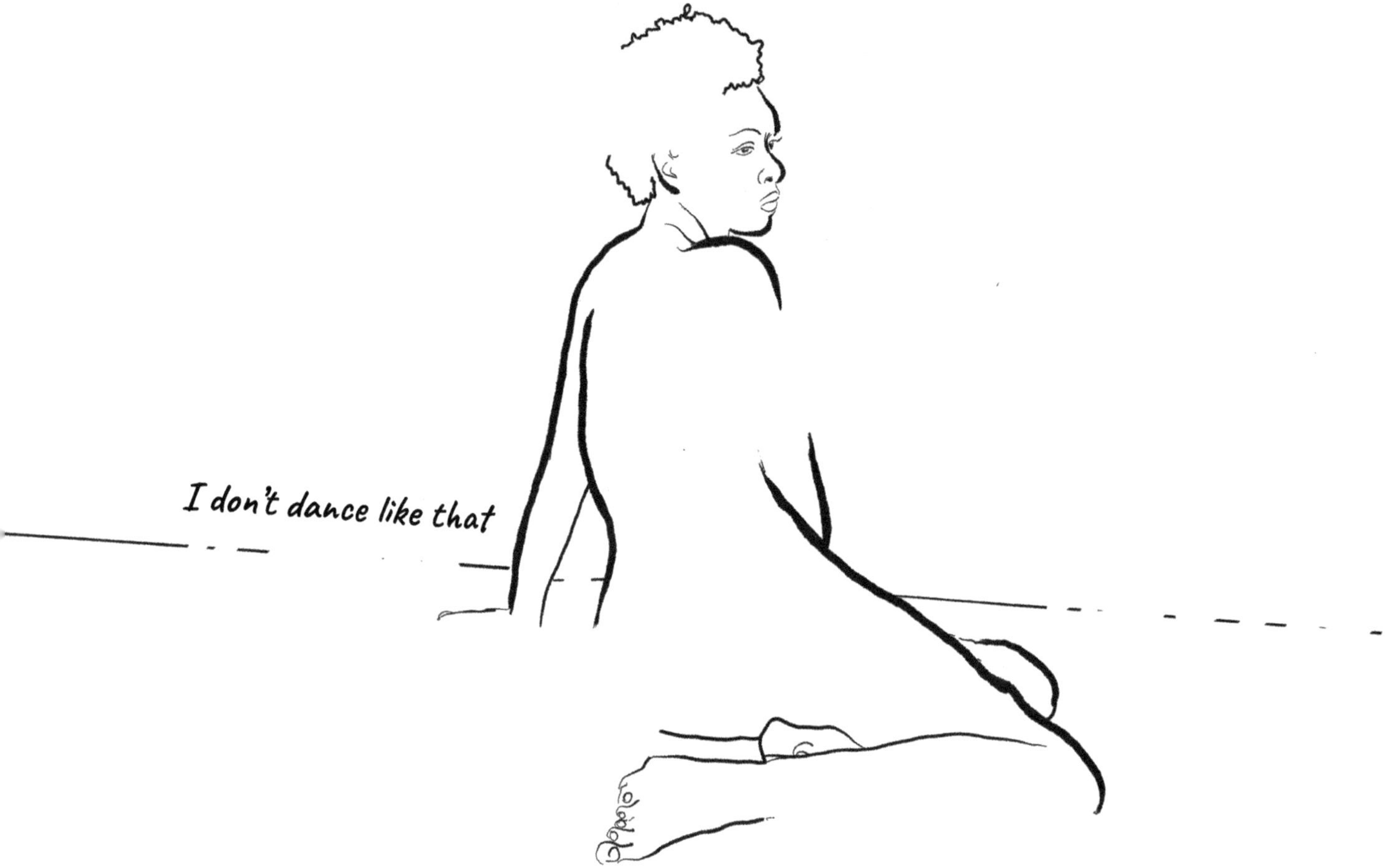

I don't dance like that

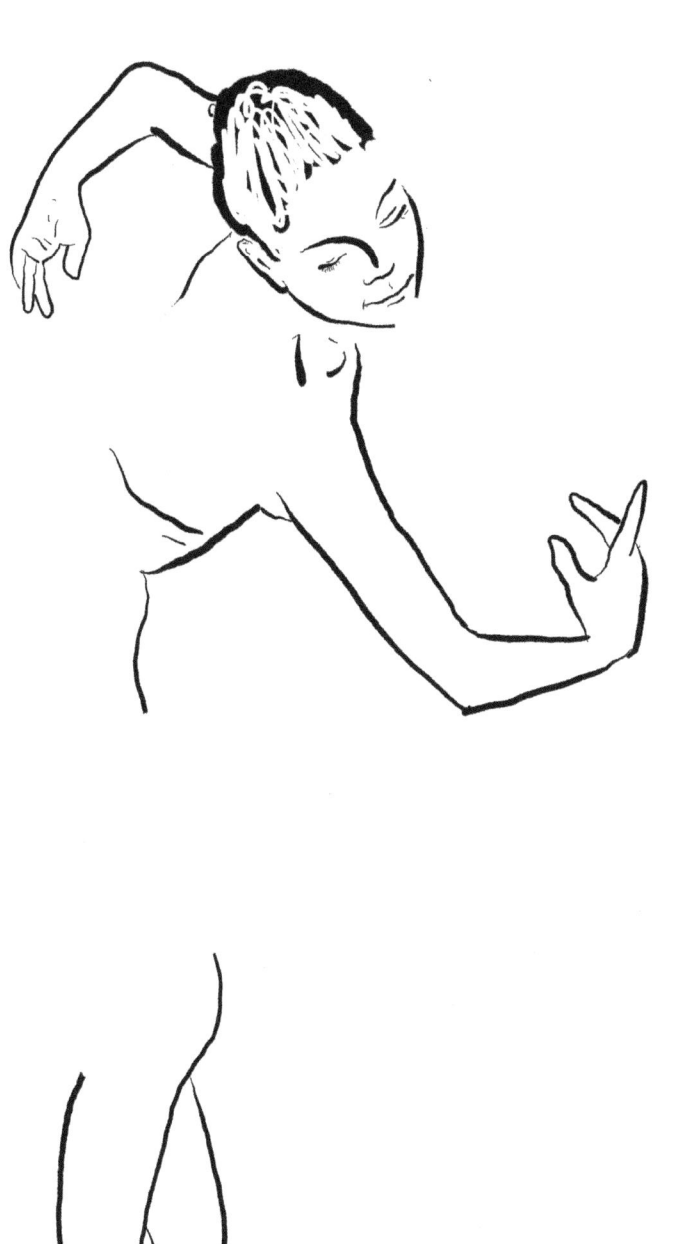

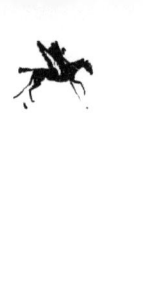

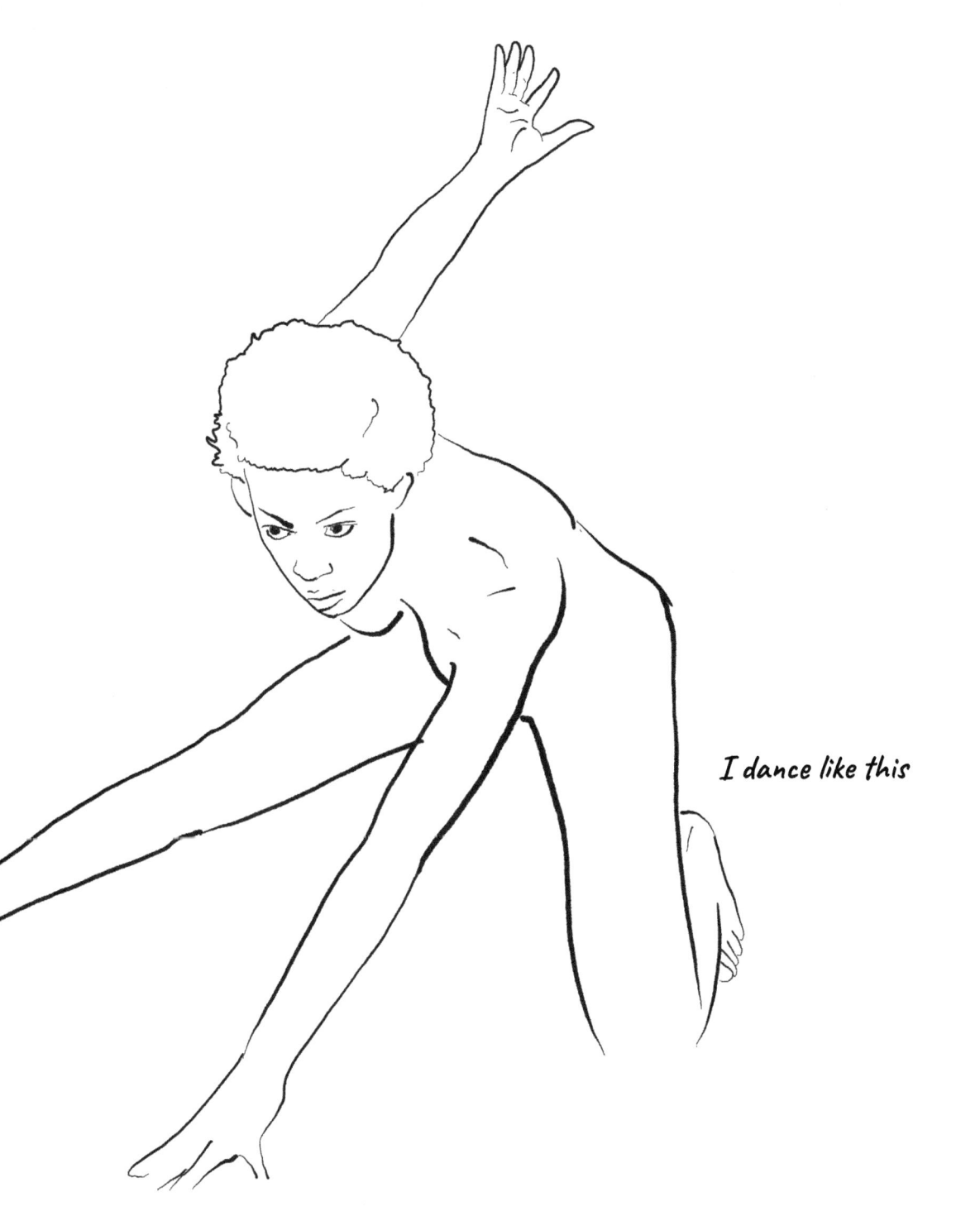

I dance like this

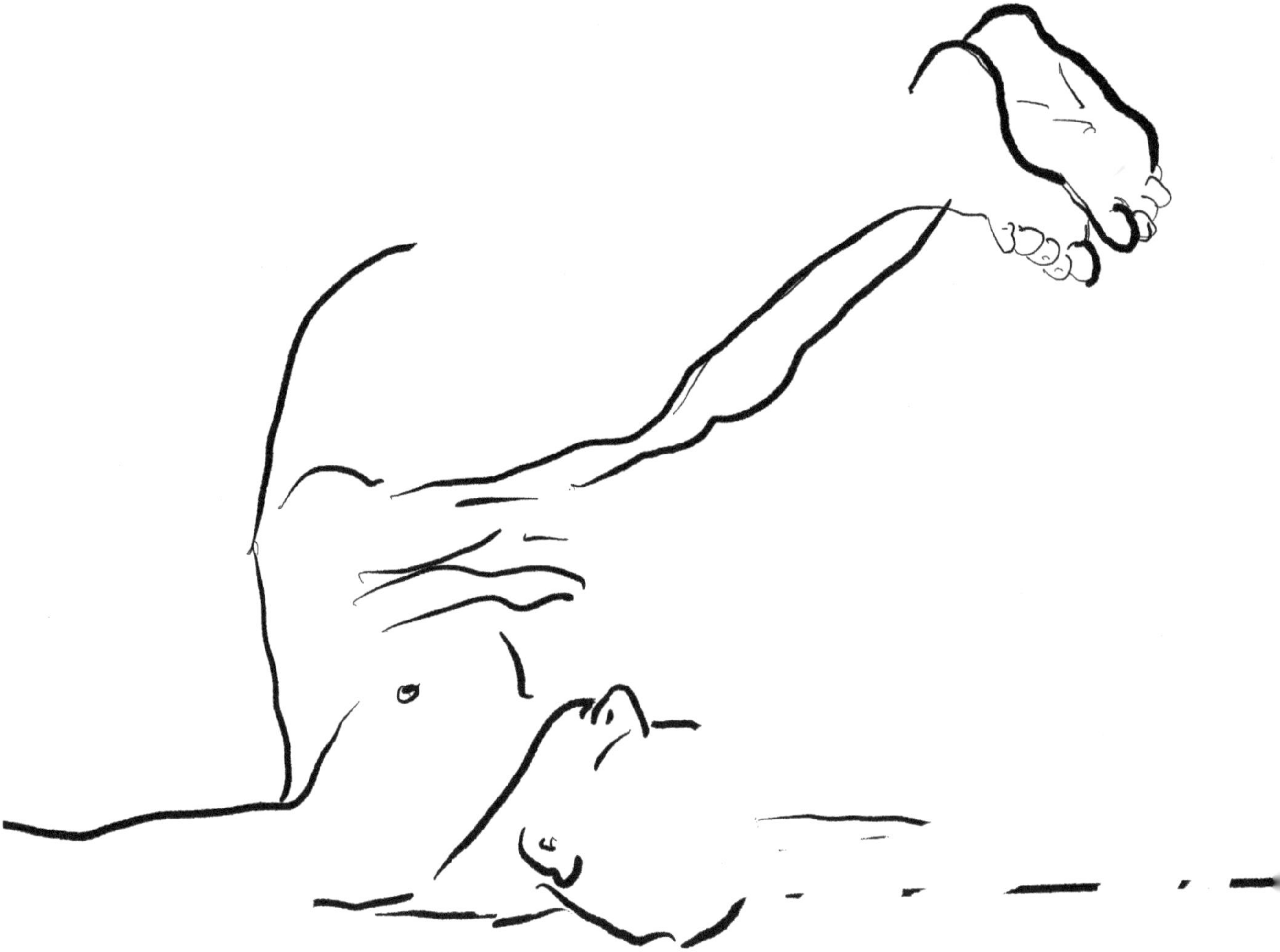

——— *More sun*

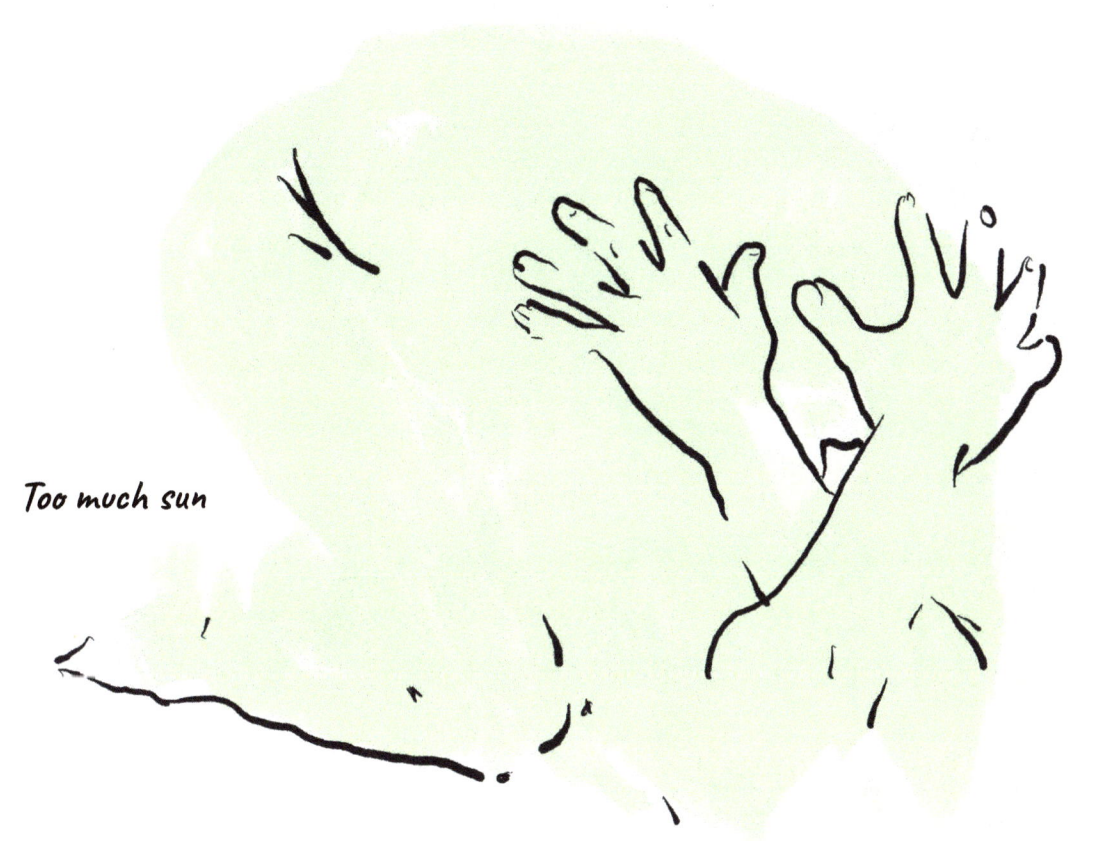

Too much sun

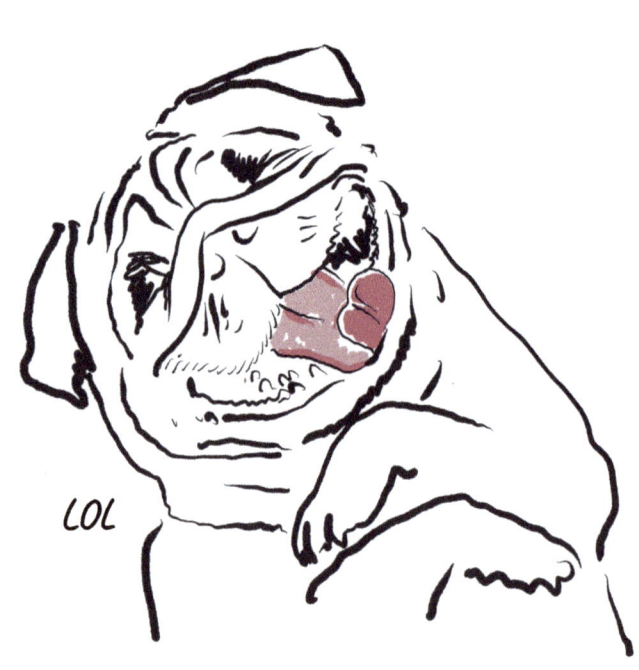

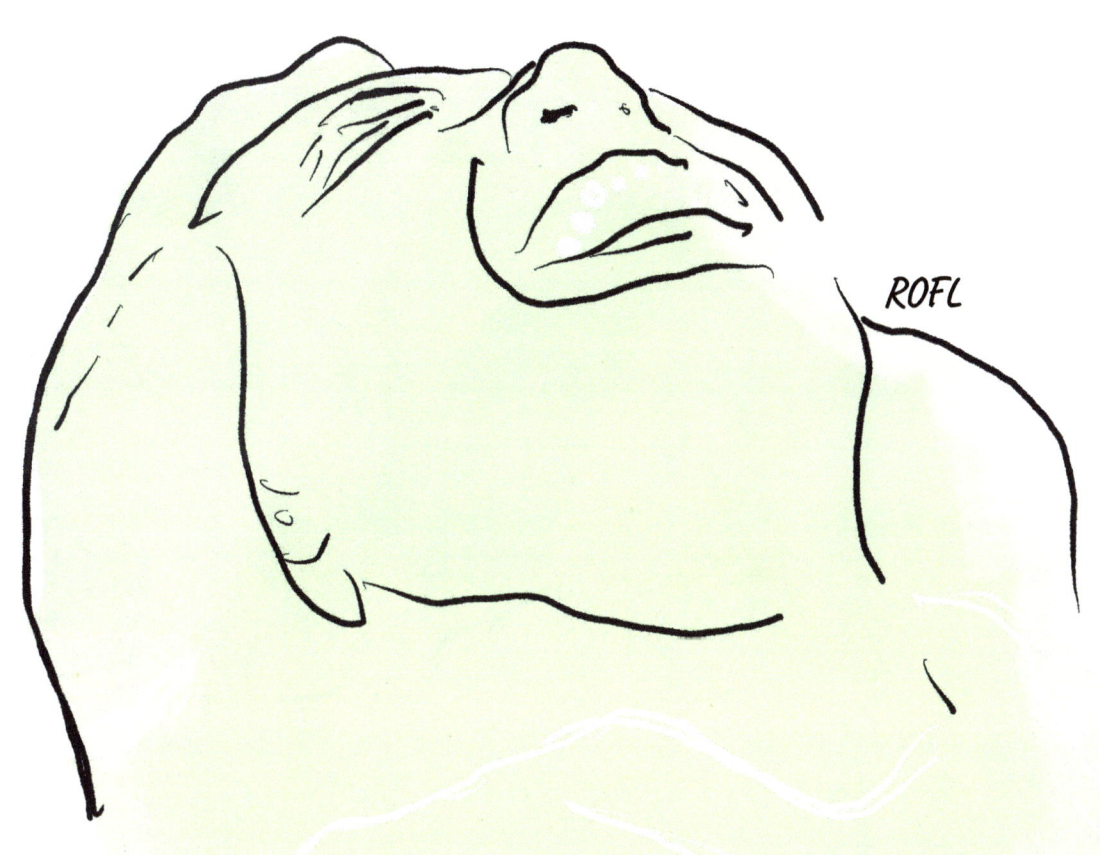

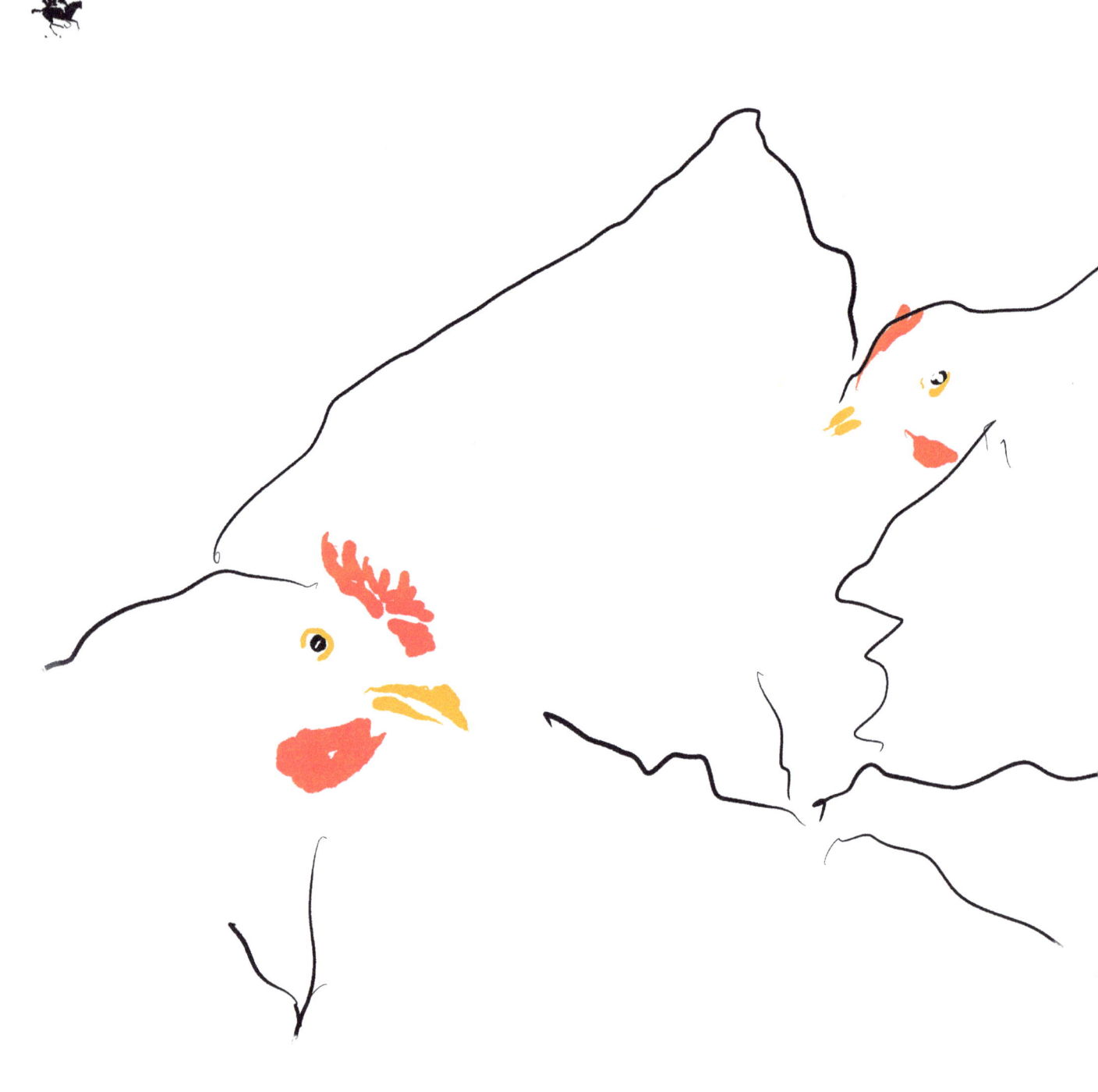

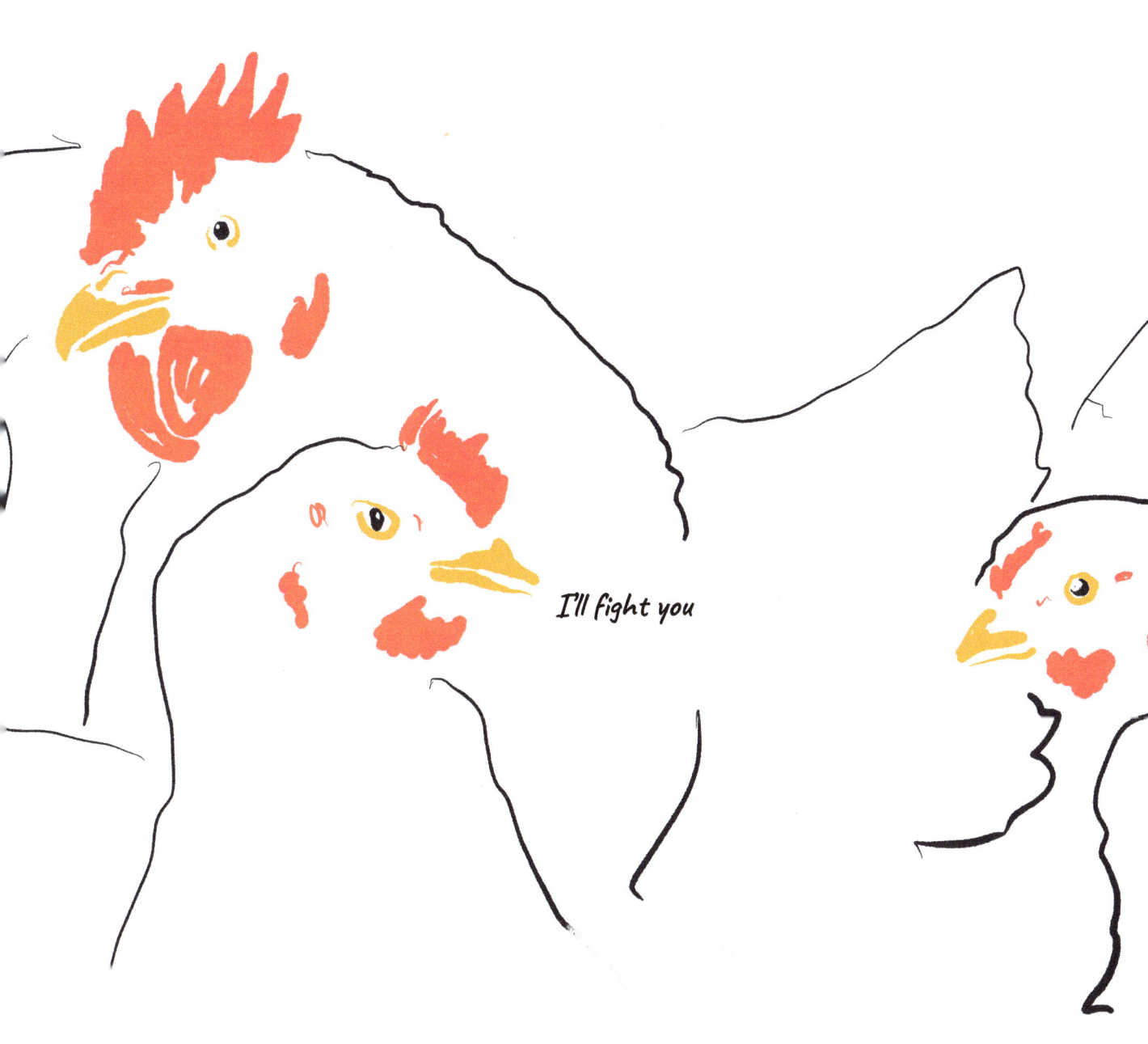

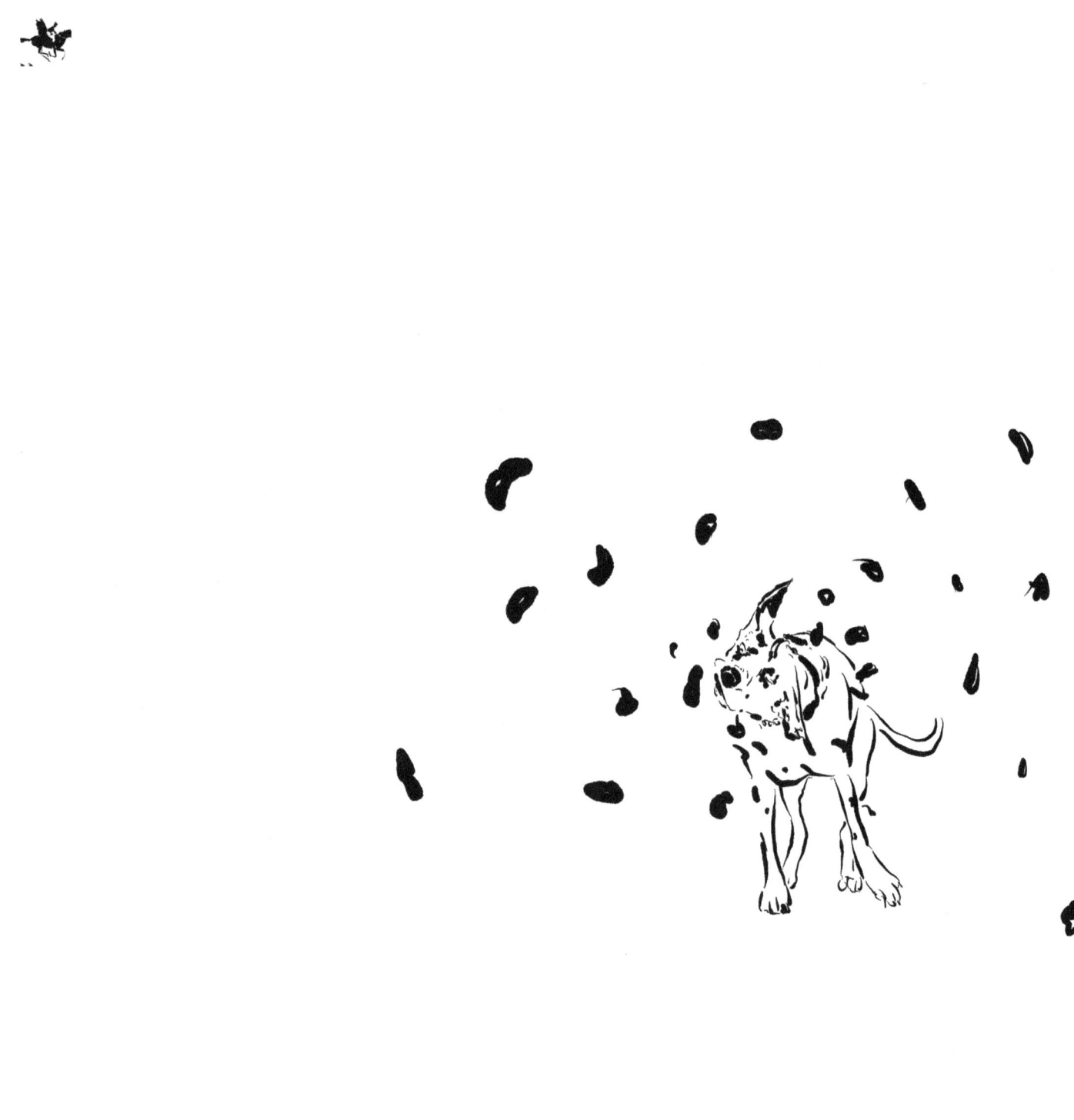

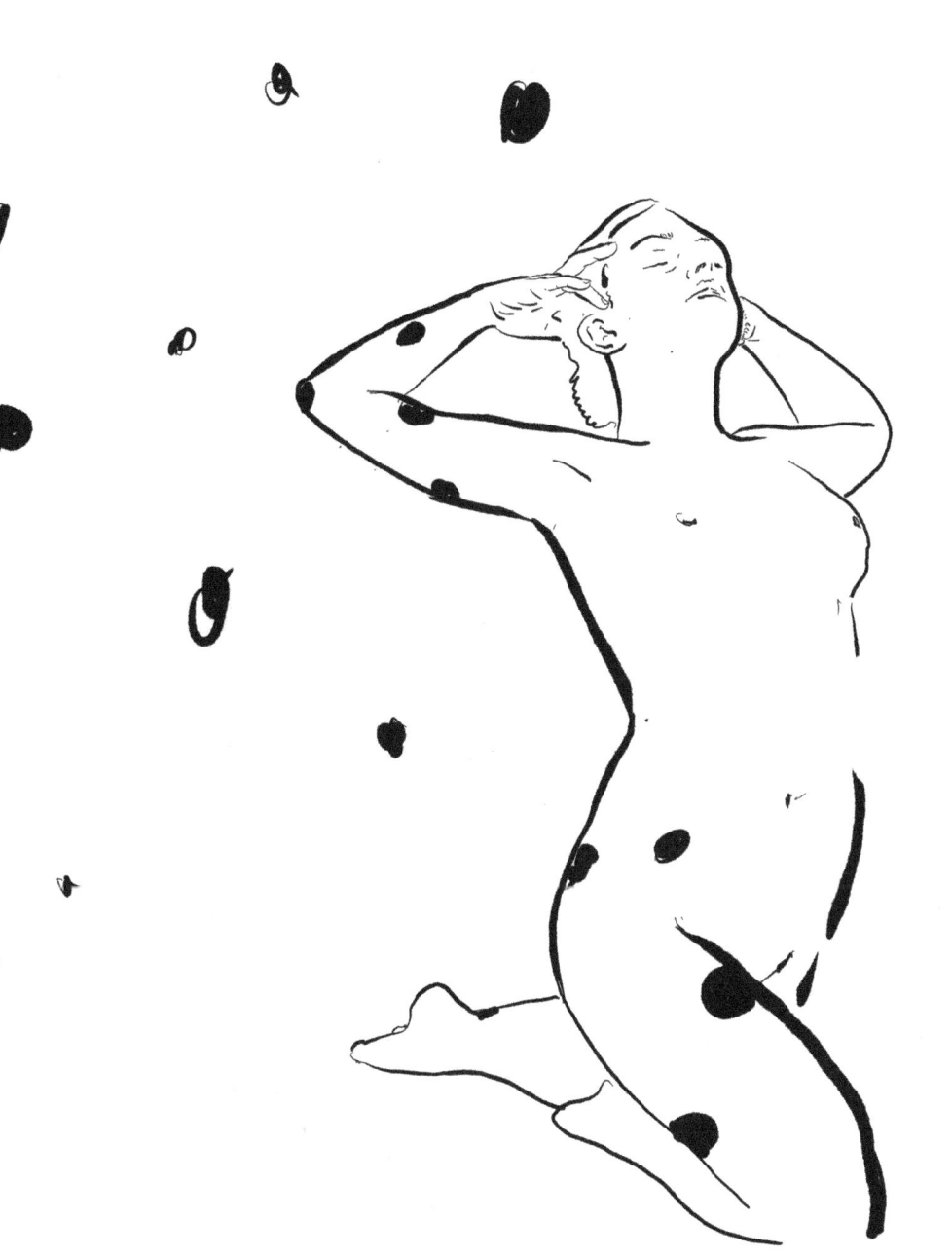

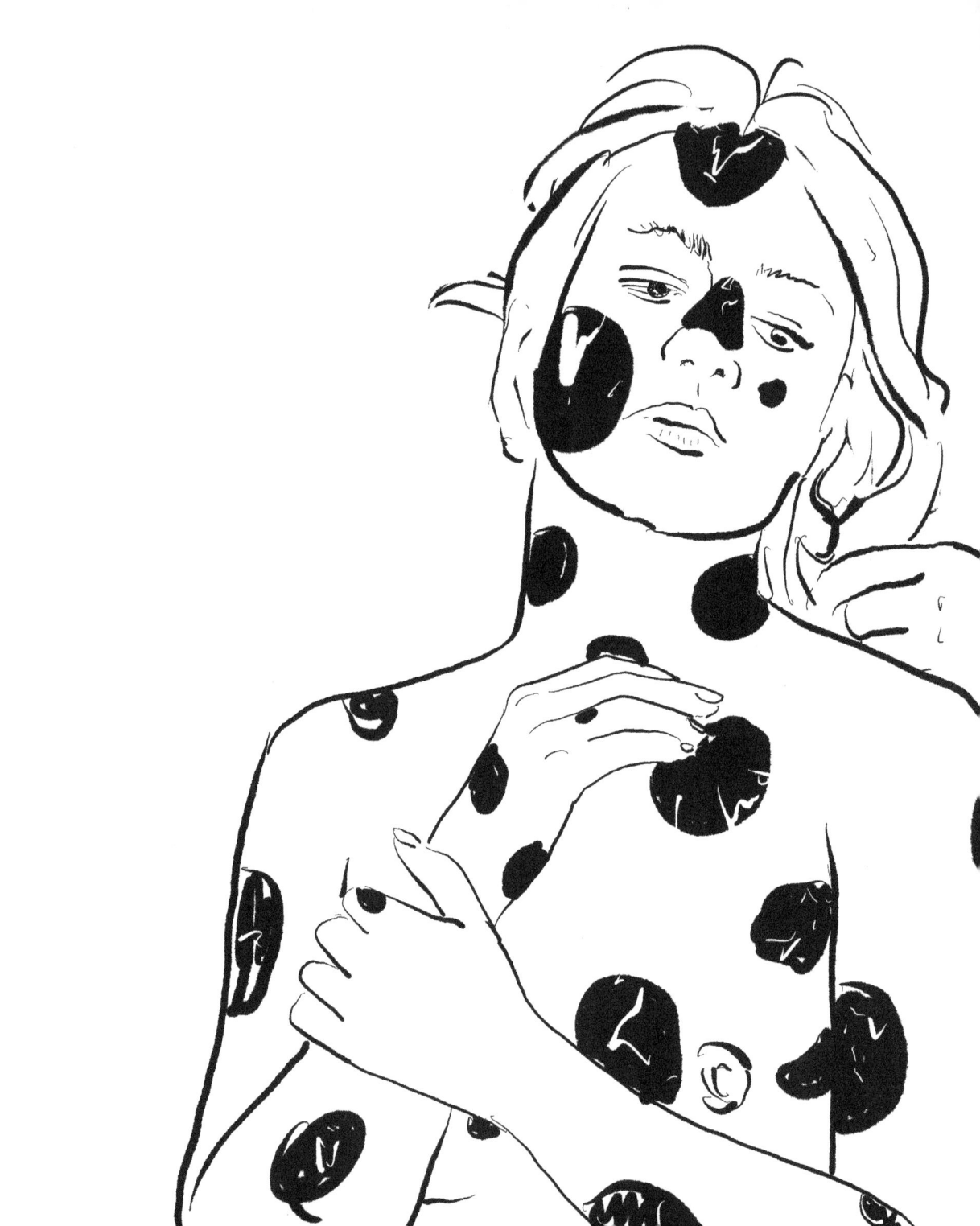

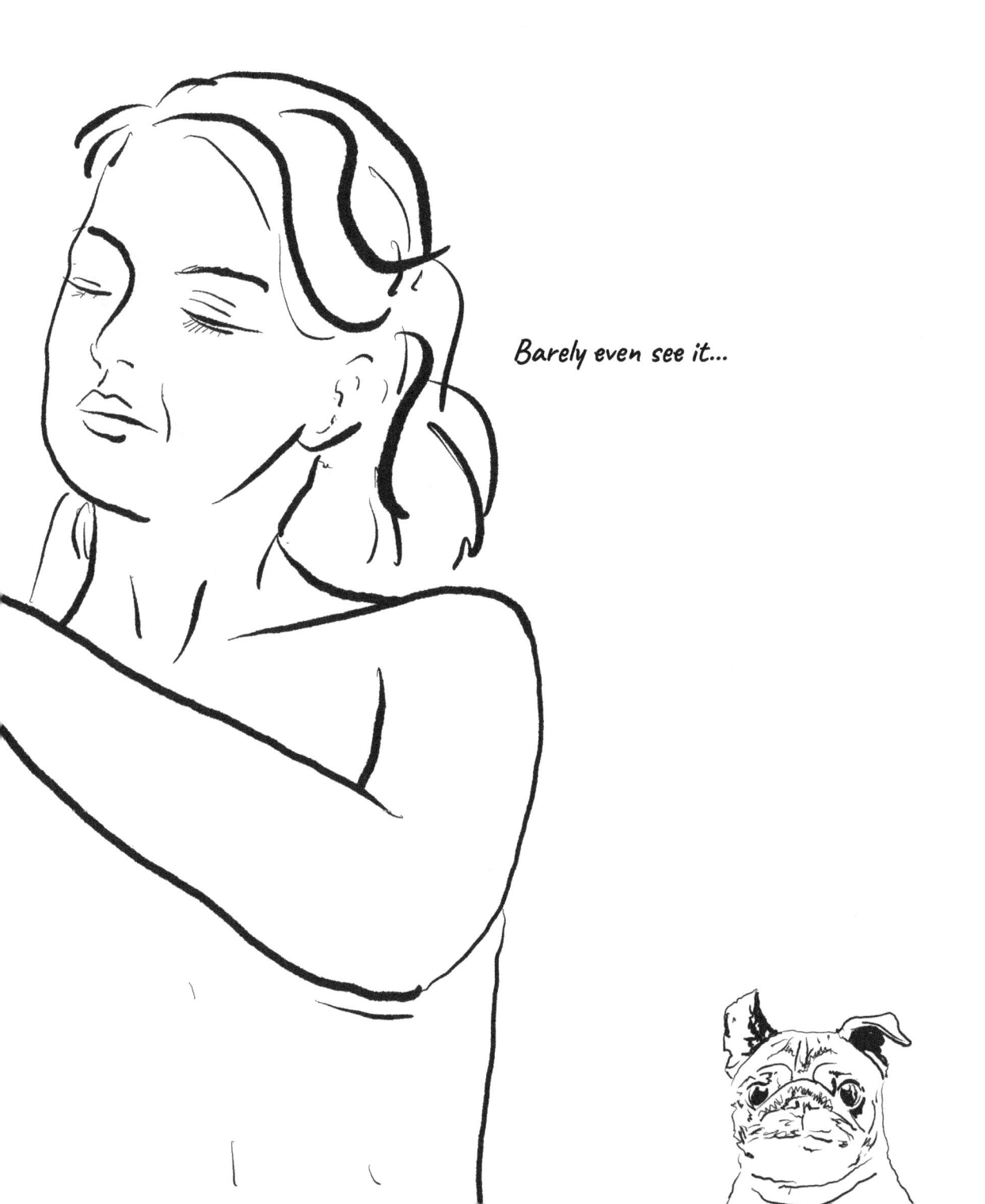

Barely even see it...

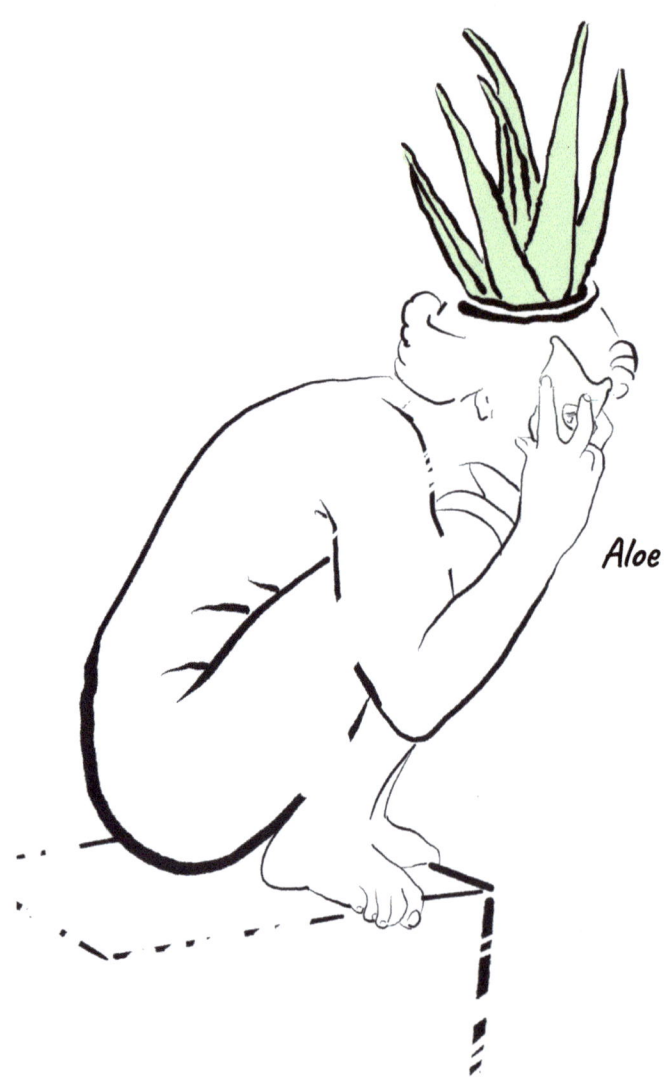

Aloe

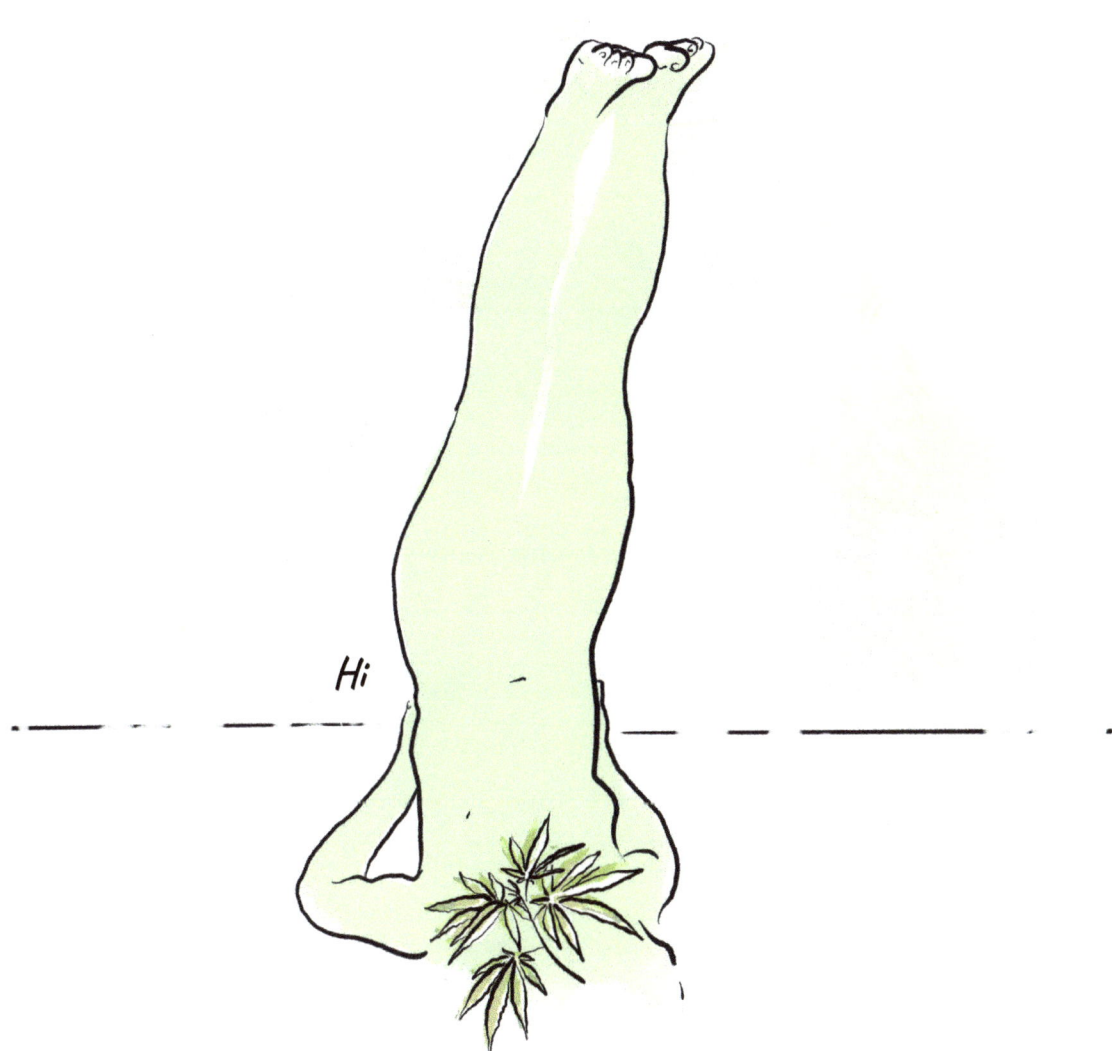

I think I got away

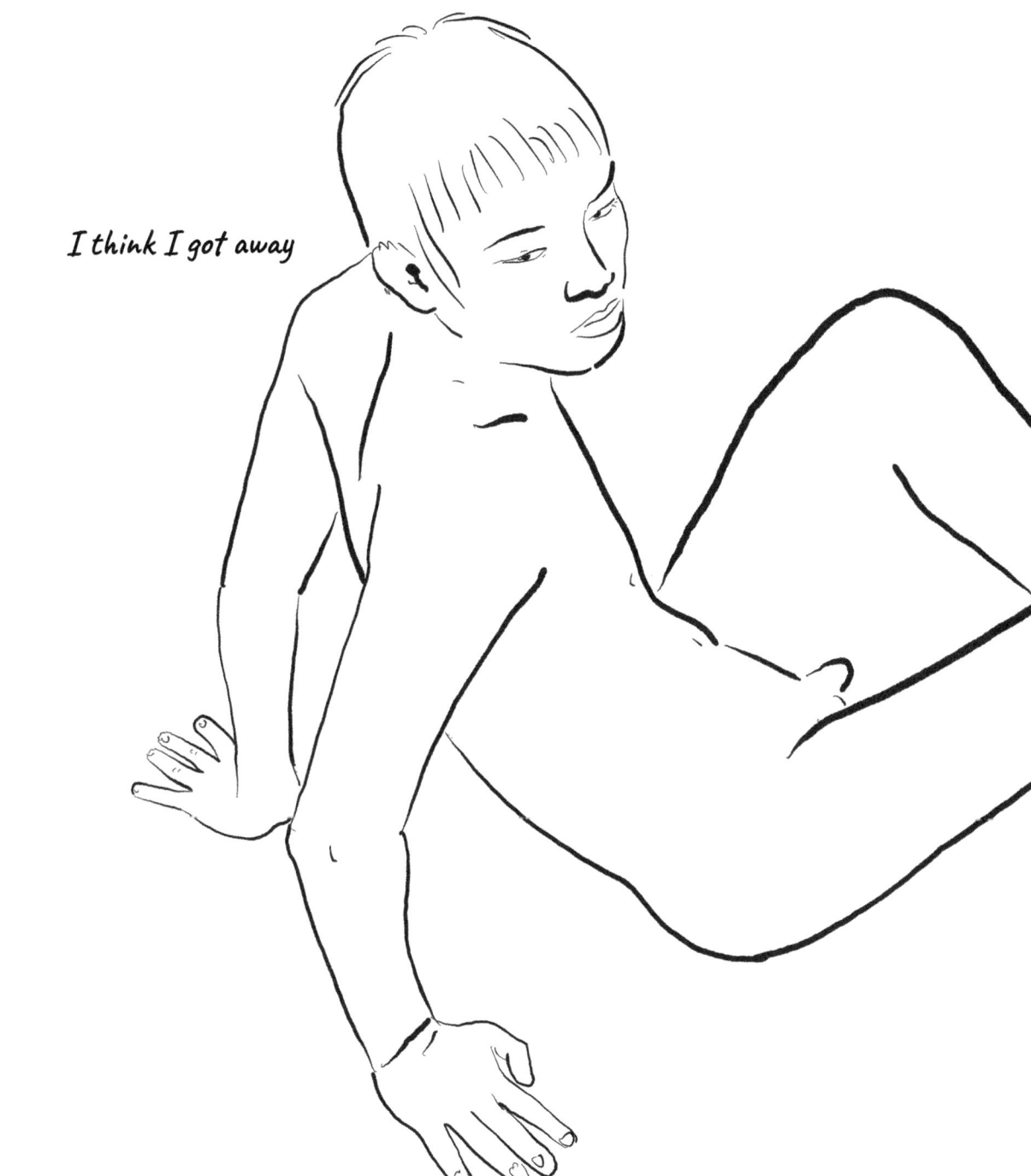

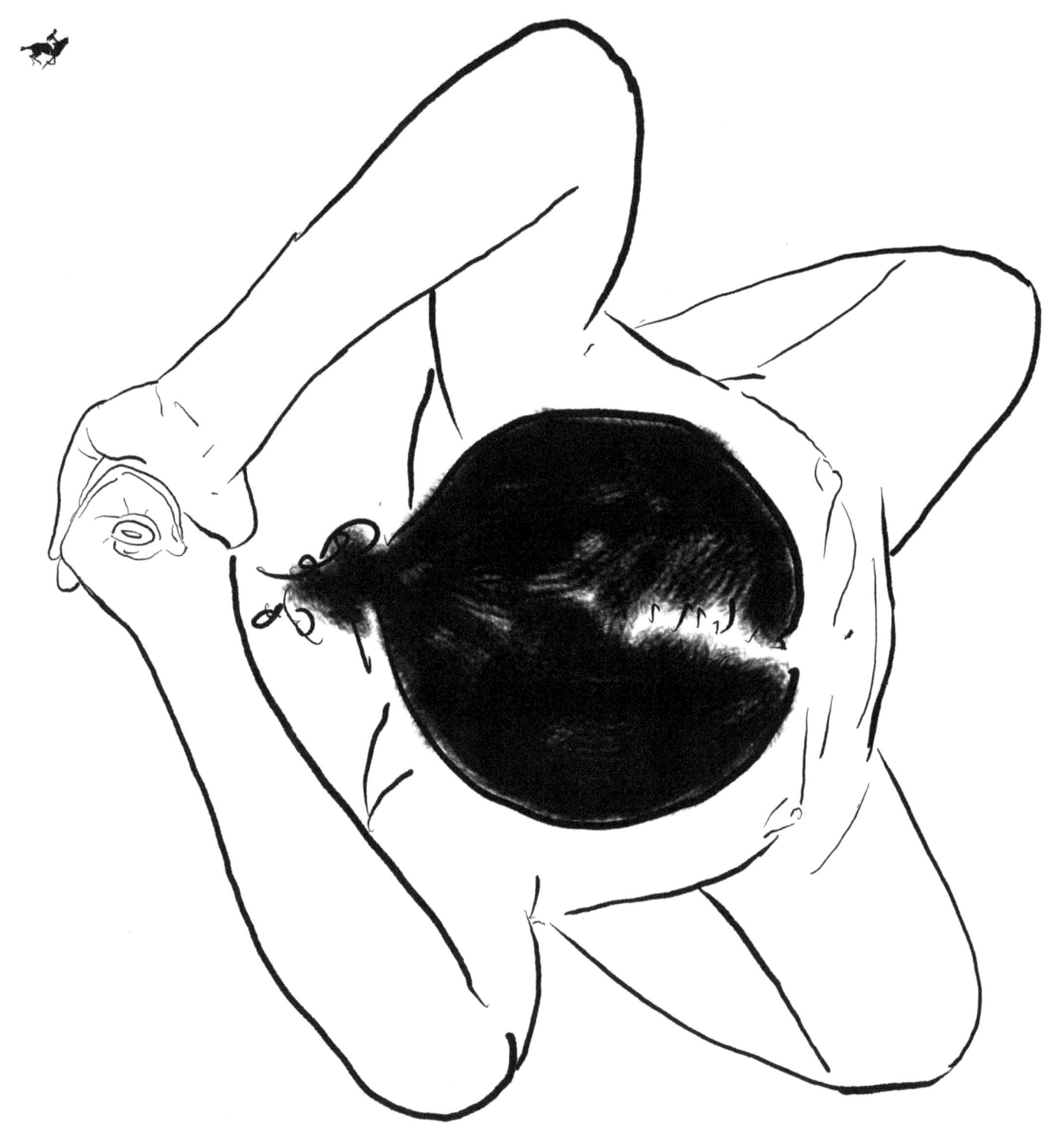

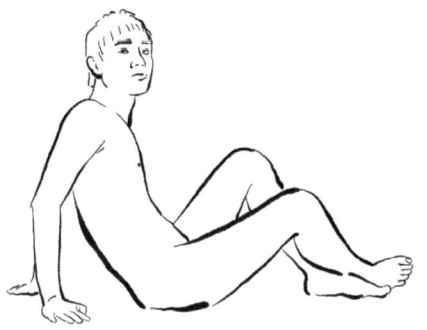

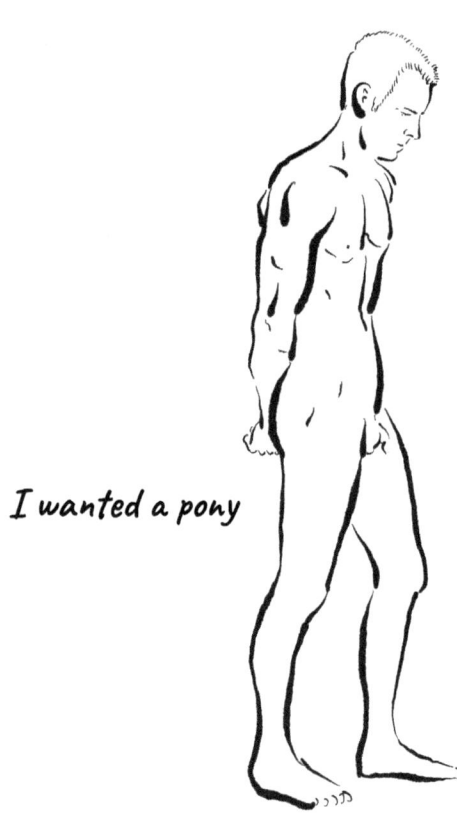

I wanted a pony

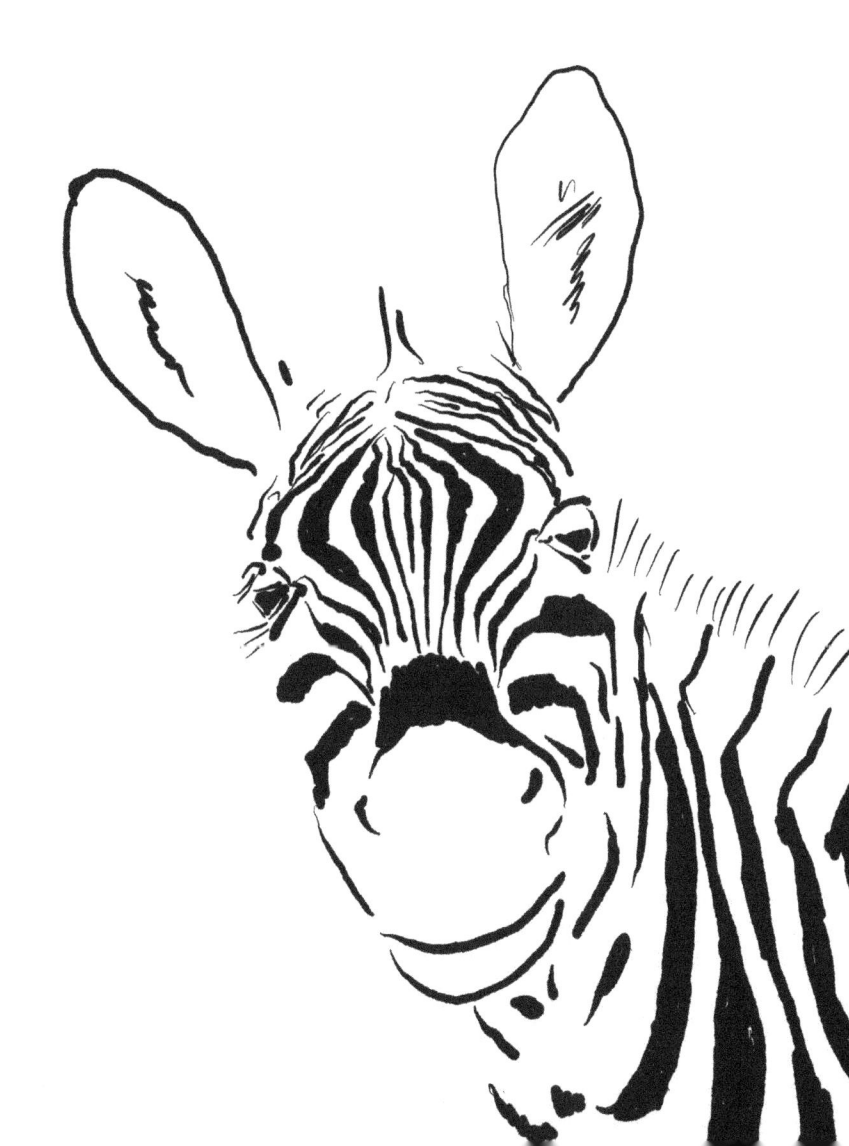

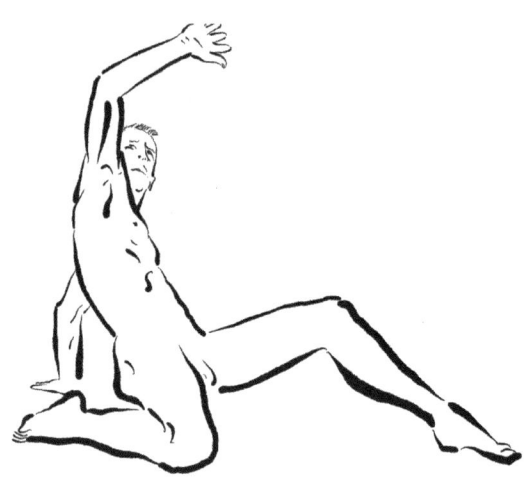

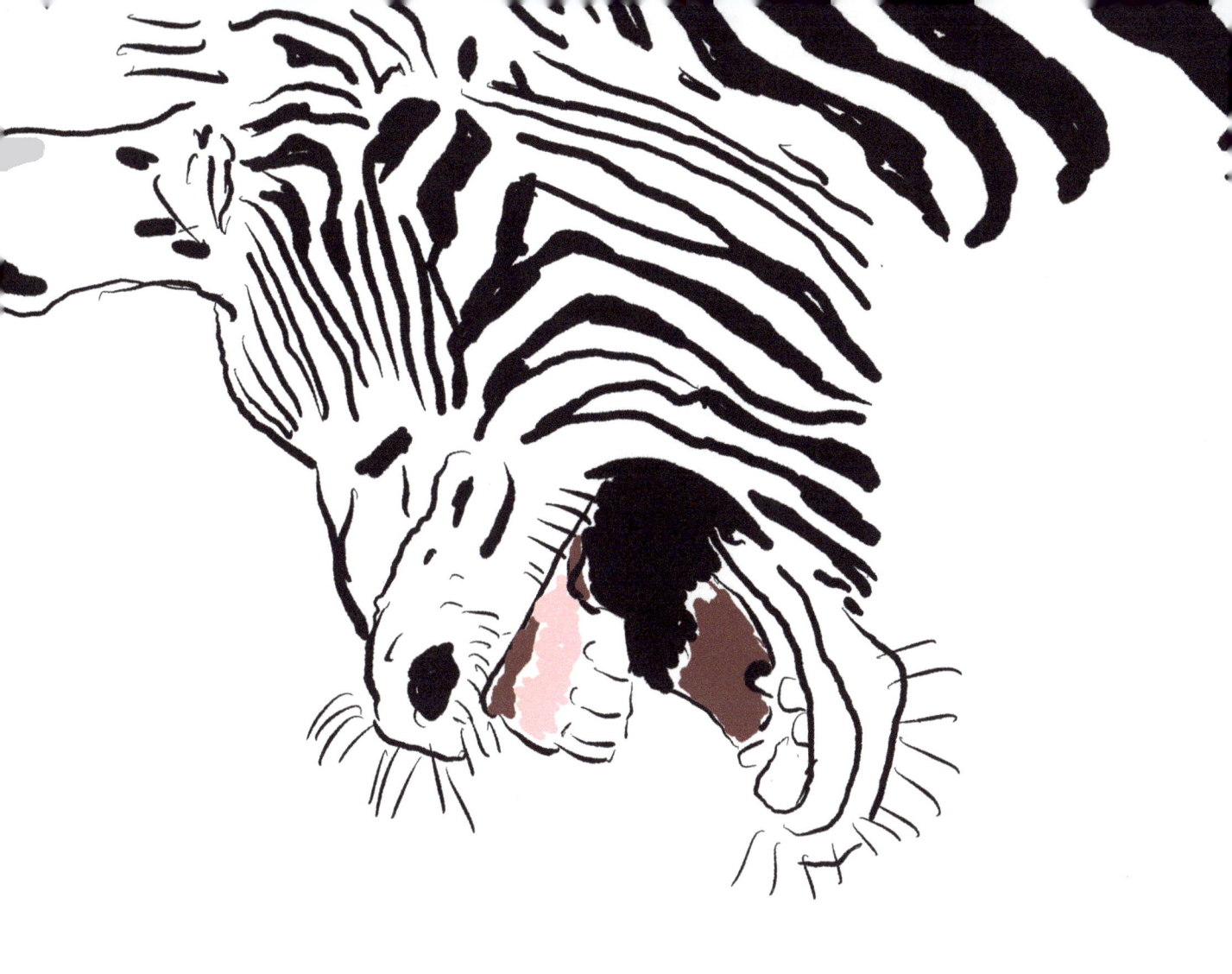

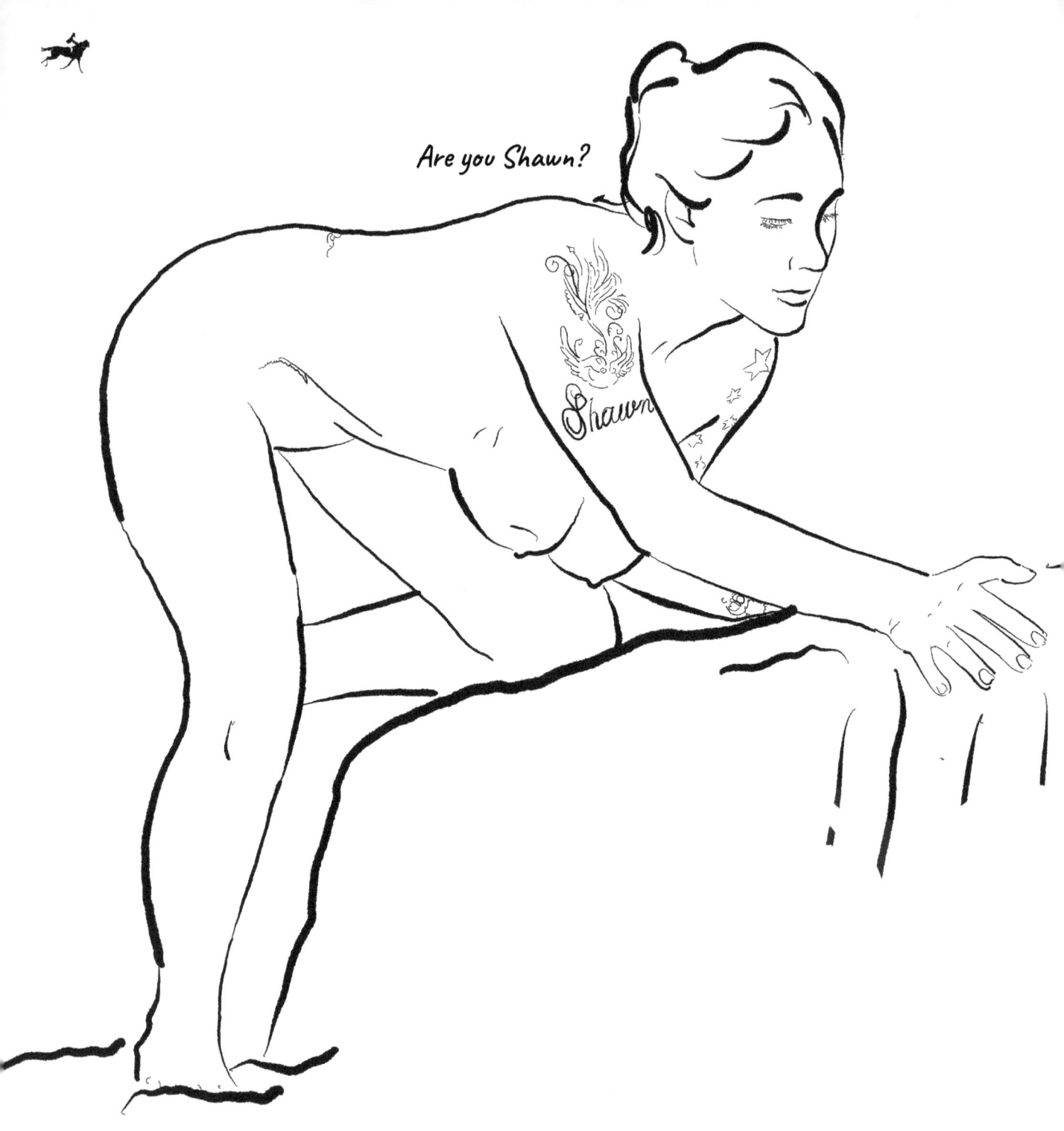

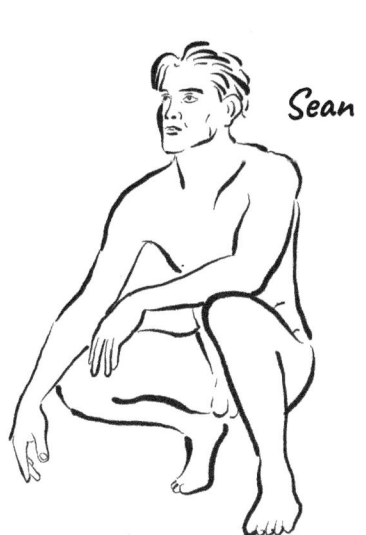

Sean

3.14159265358979323846264338327950288419716939937510582097494459230781640628620899

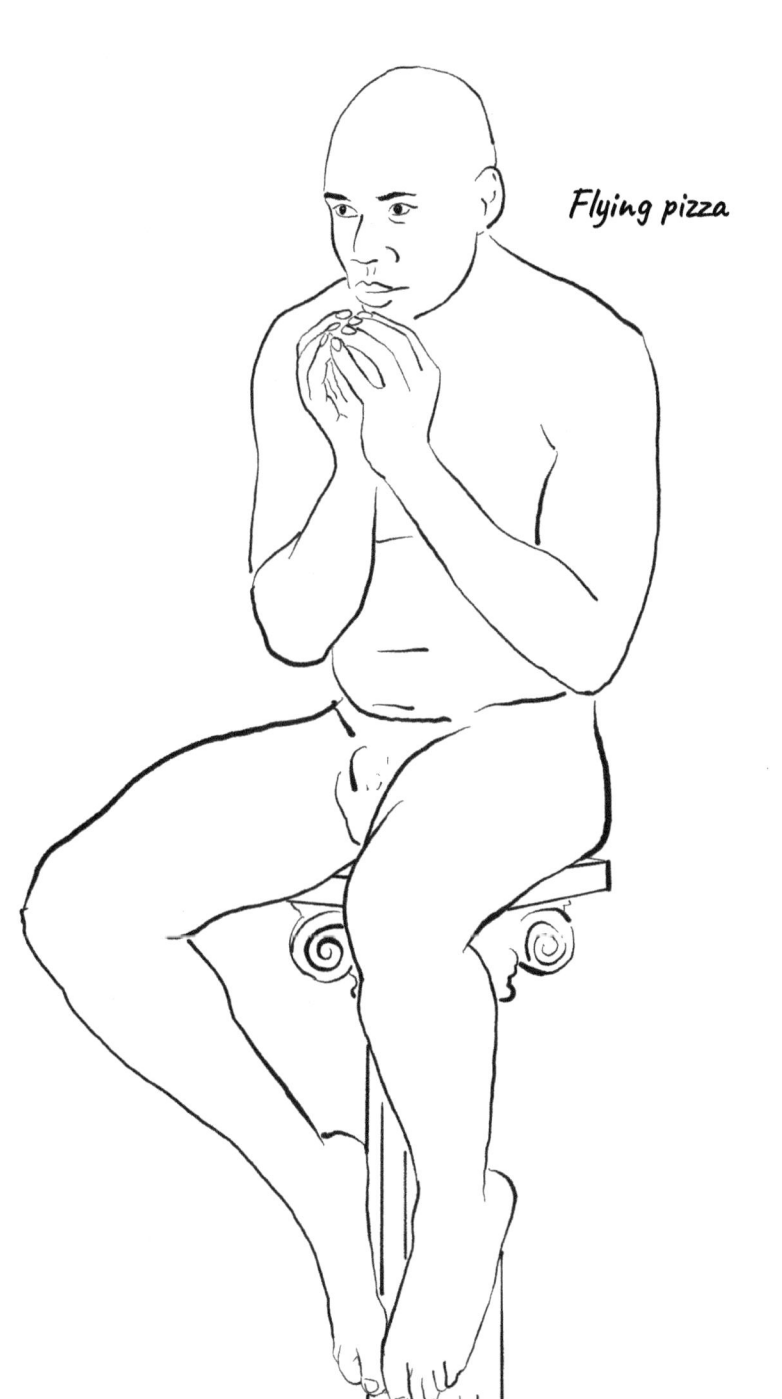

Flying pizza

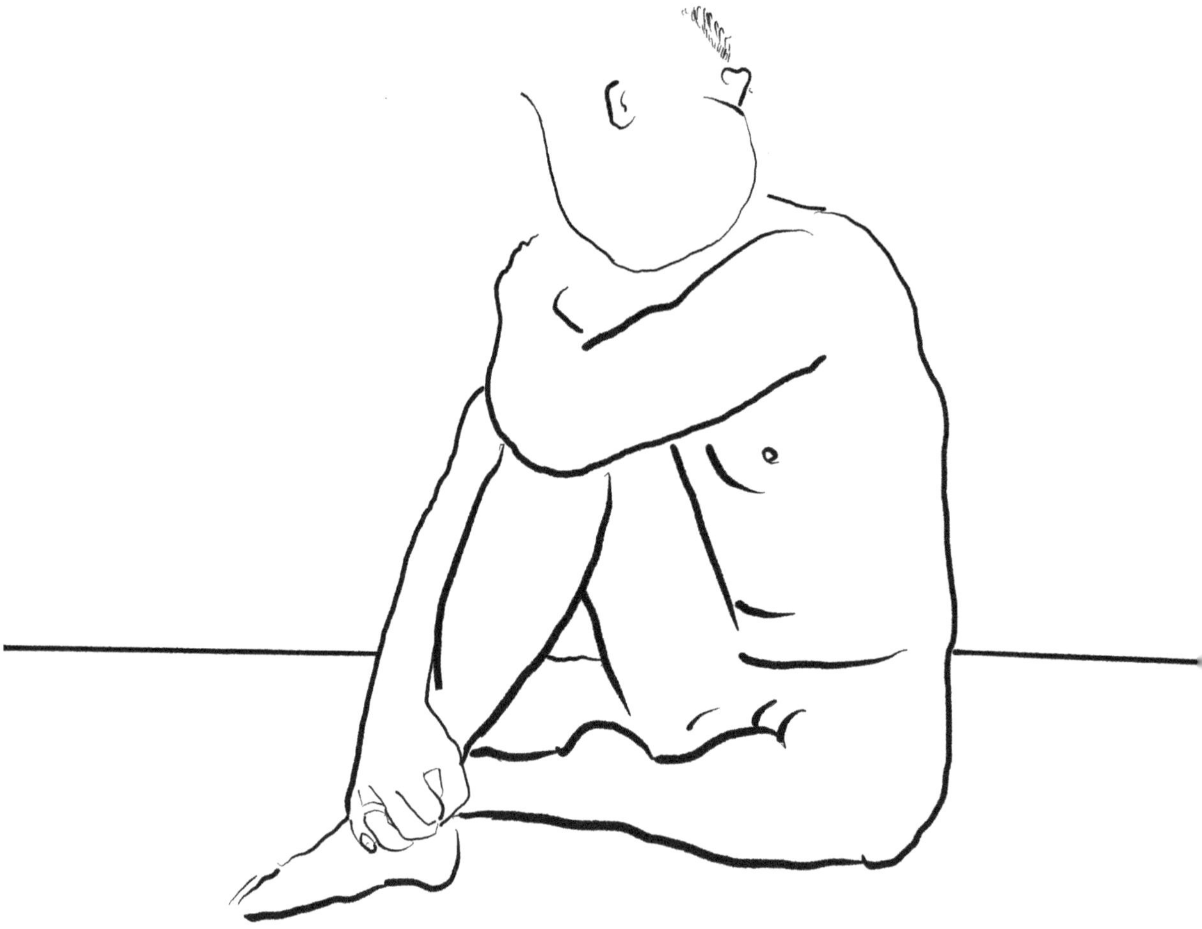

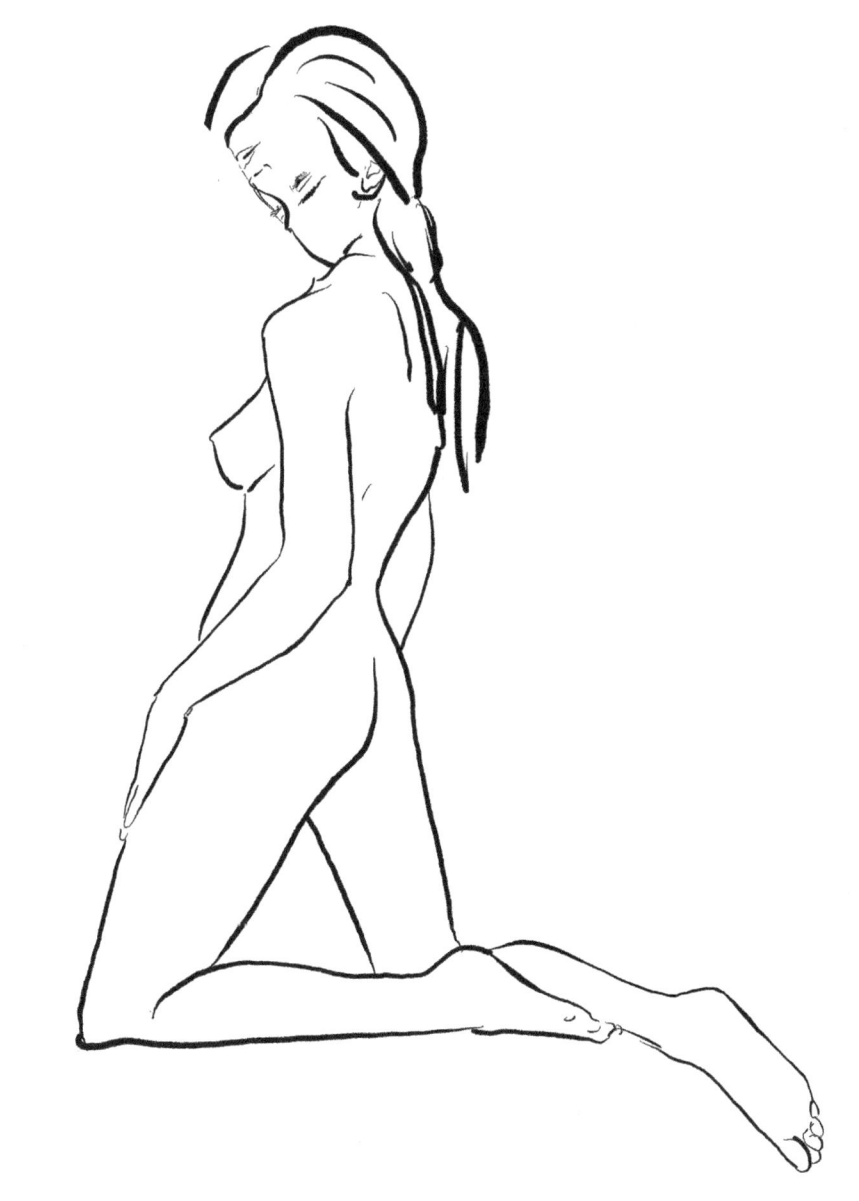

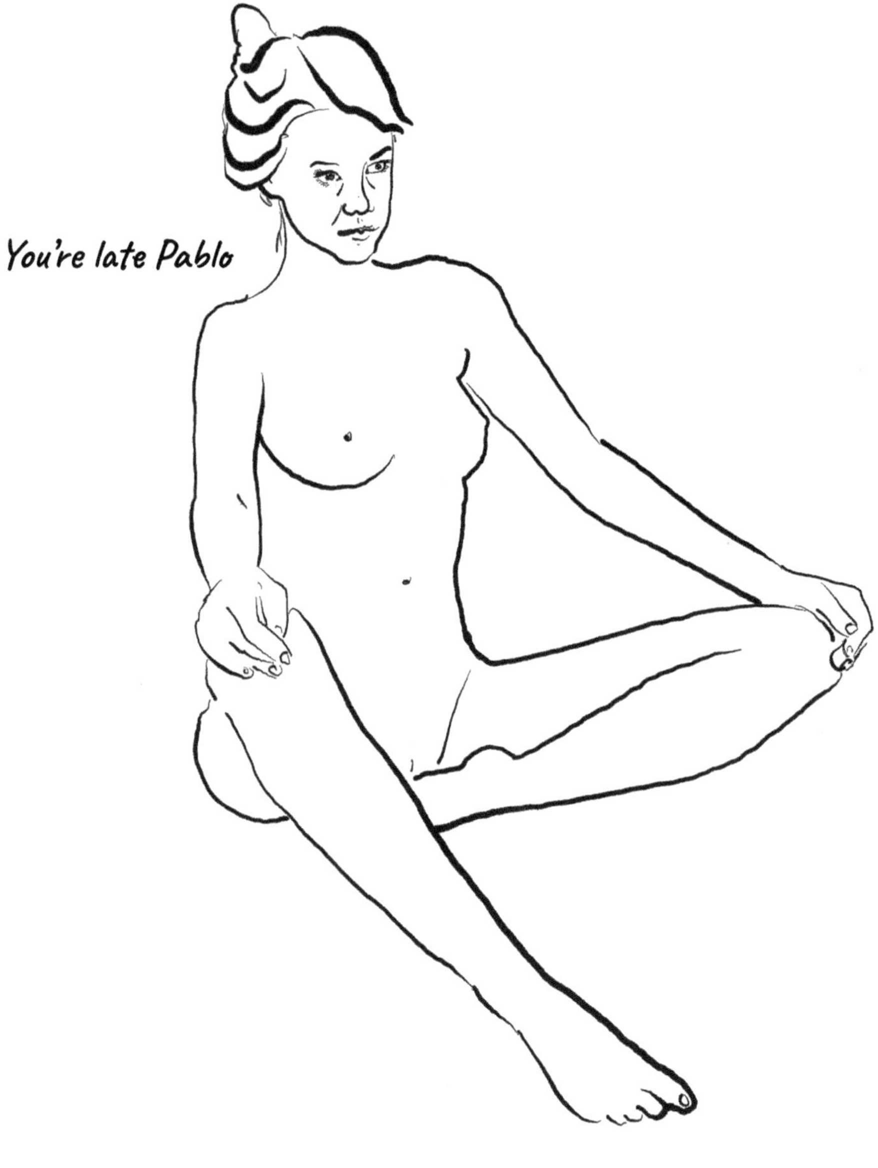

You're late Pablo

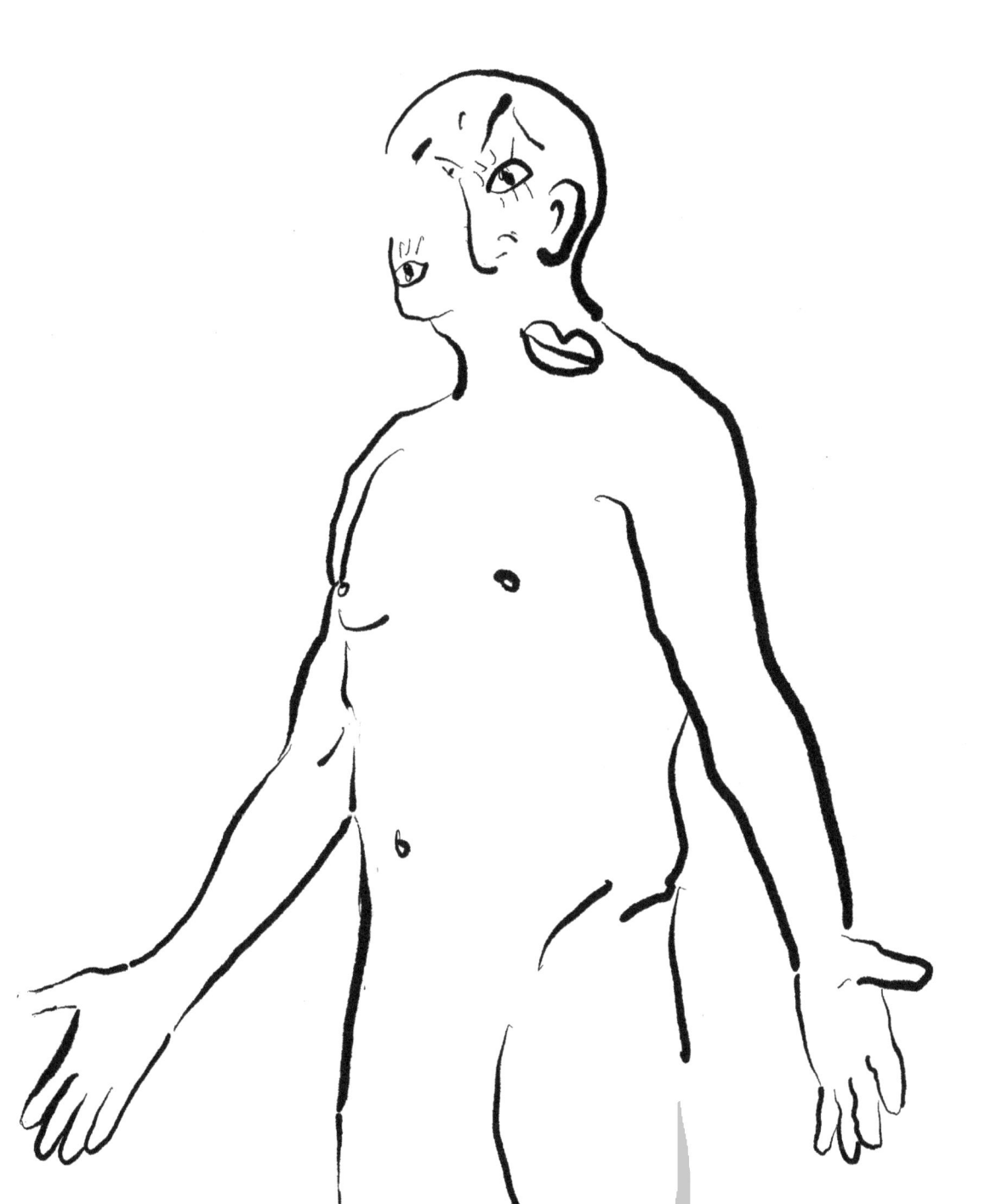

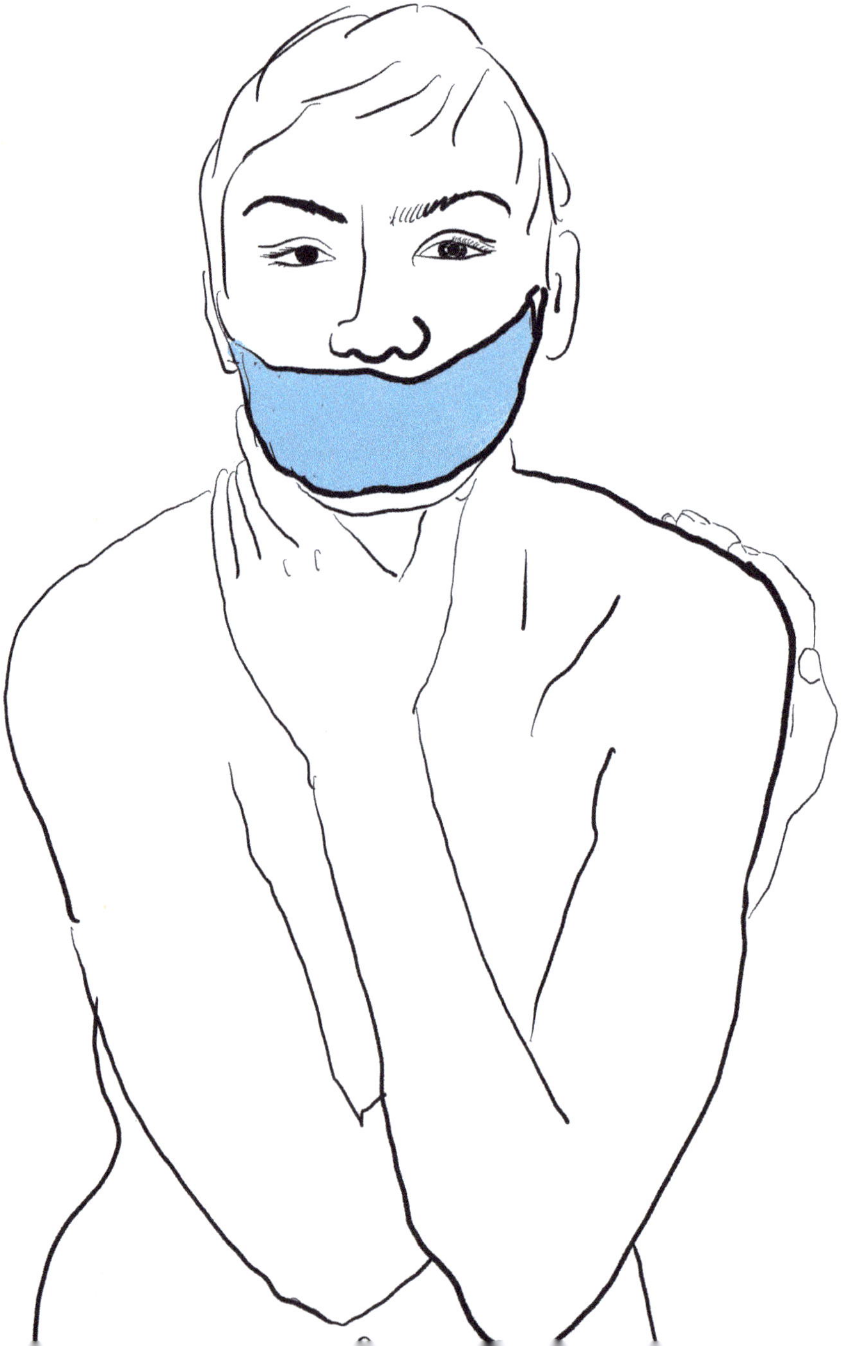

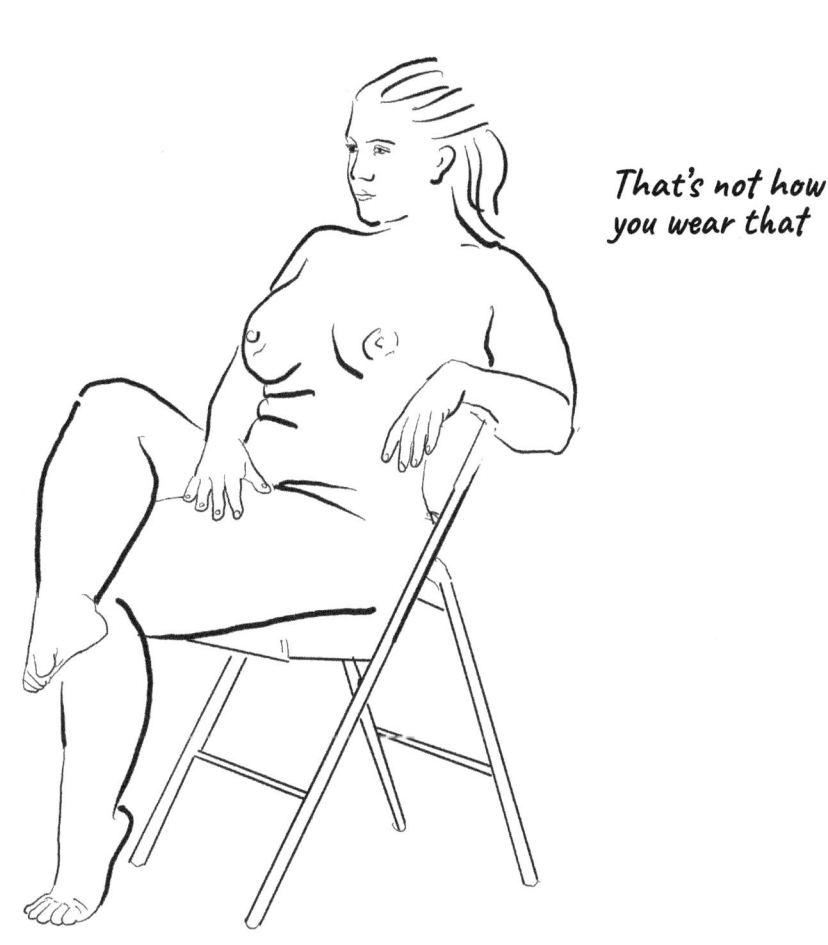

That's not how
you wear that

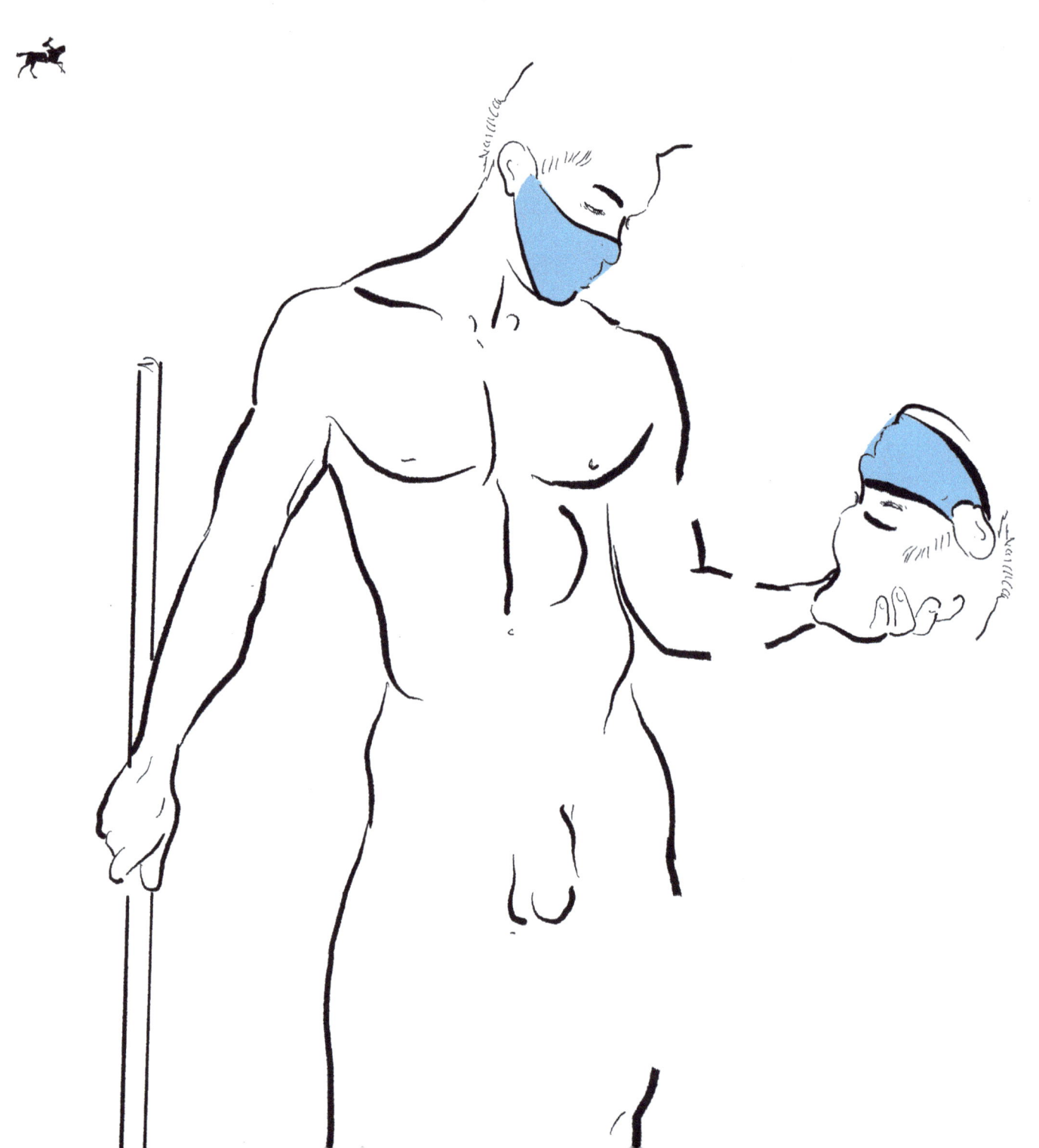

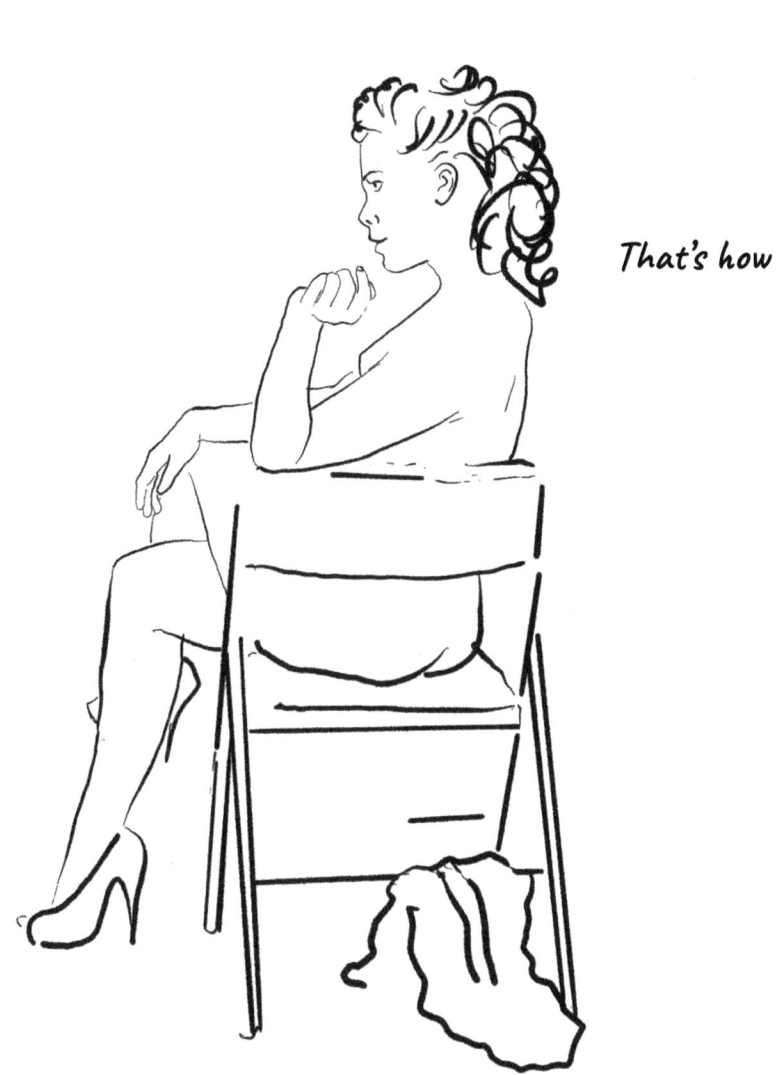

That's how

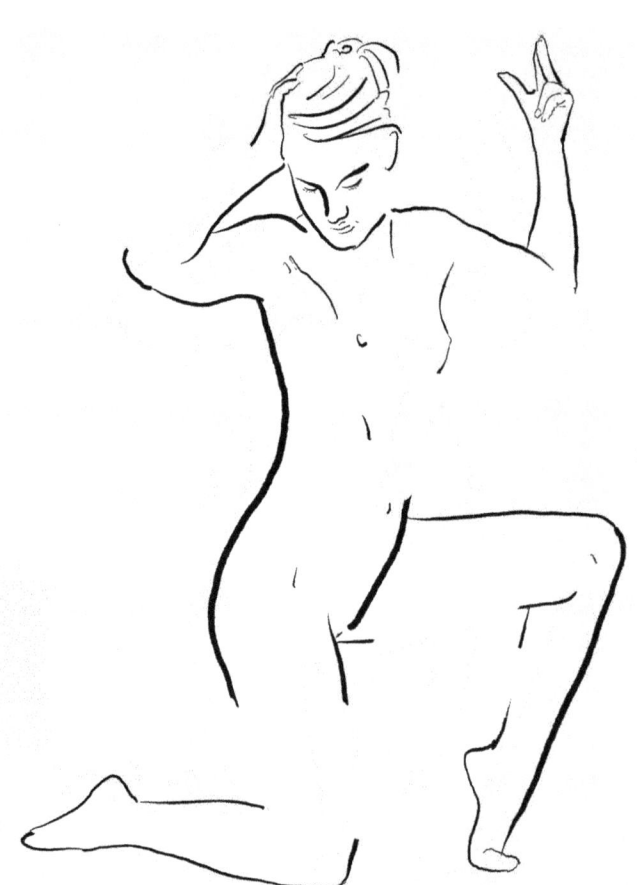

Chapter Two

Celebrity Sayings

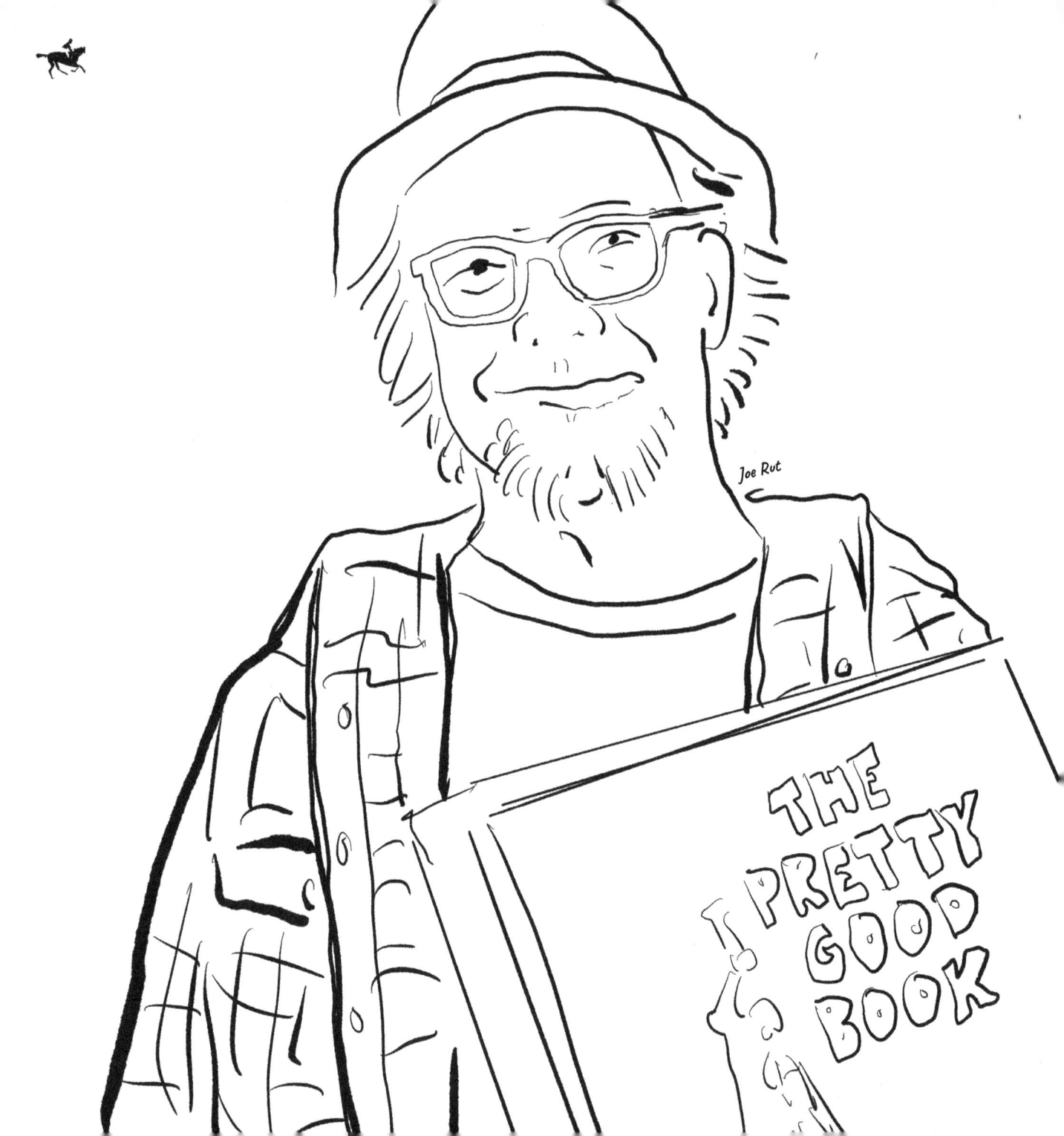

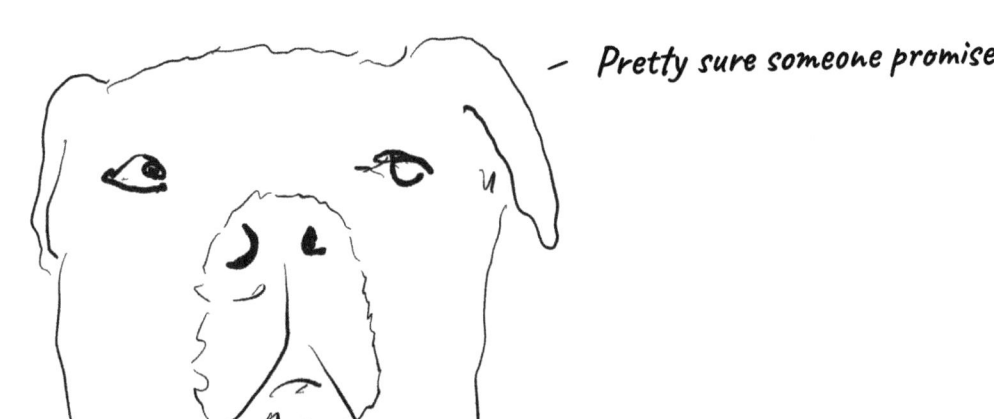

Pretty sure someone promised steak

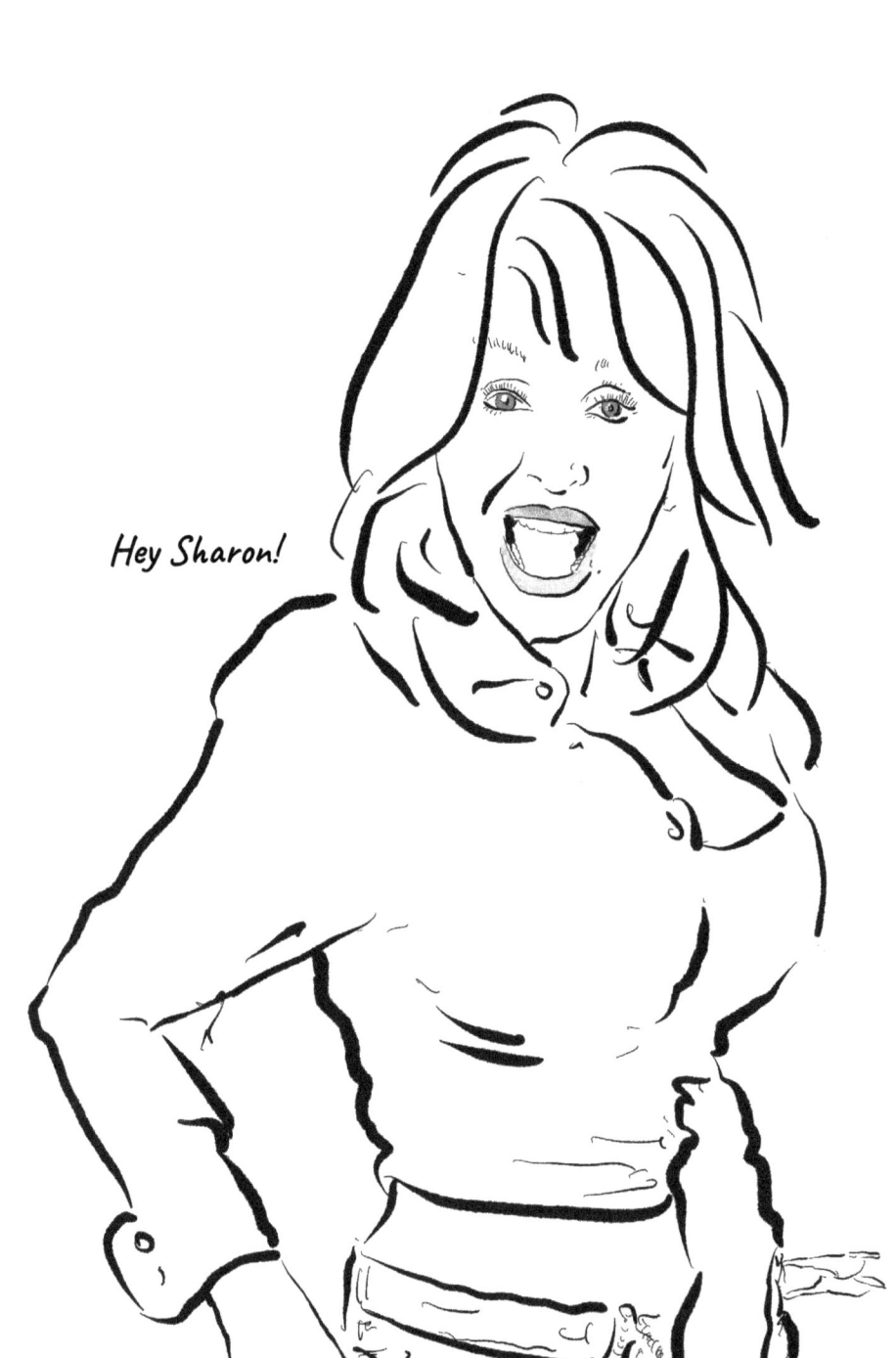

Hey Sharon!

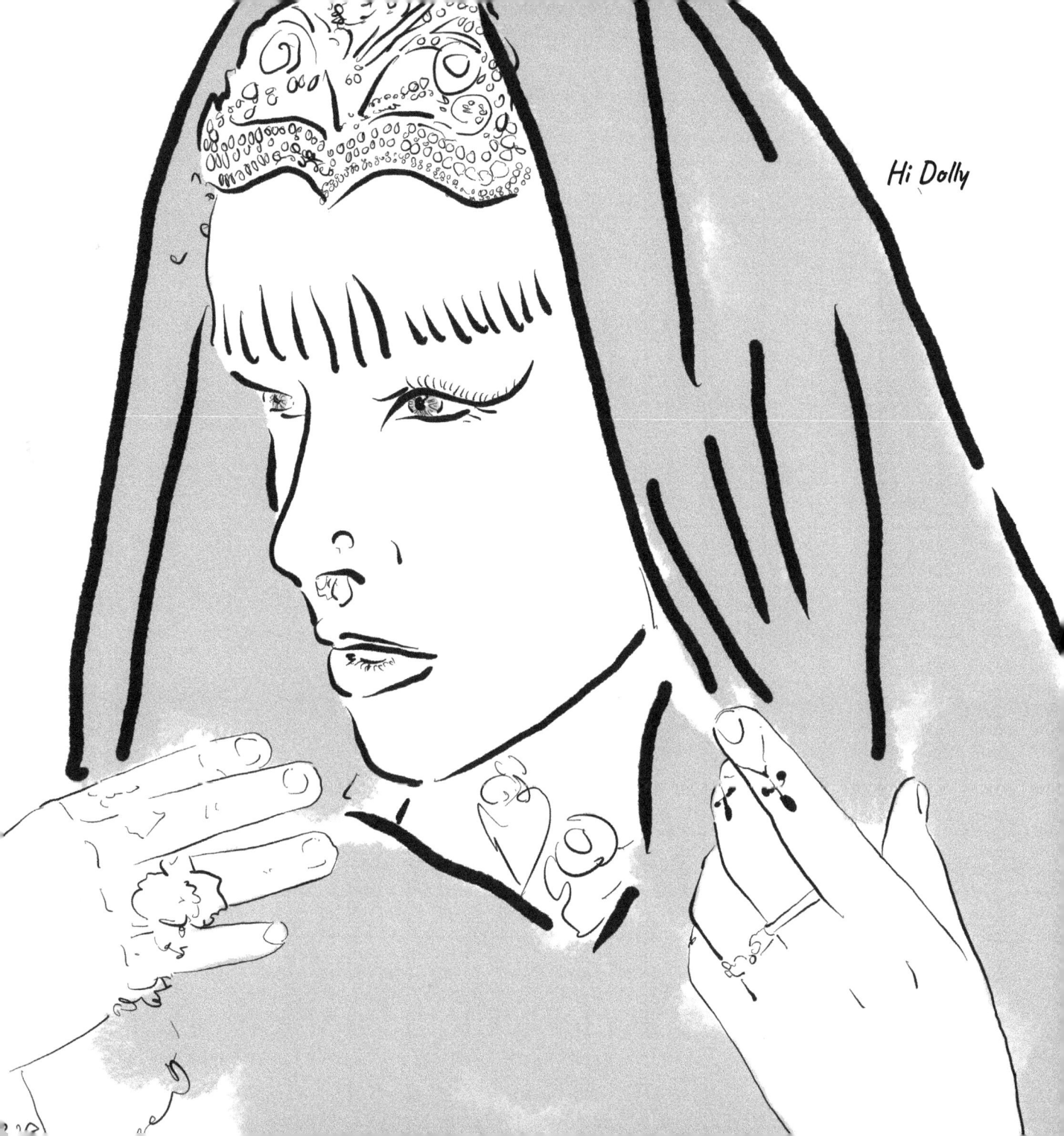

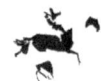

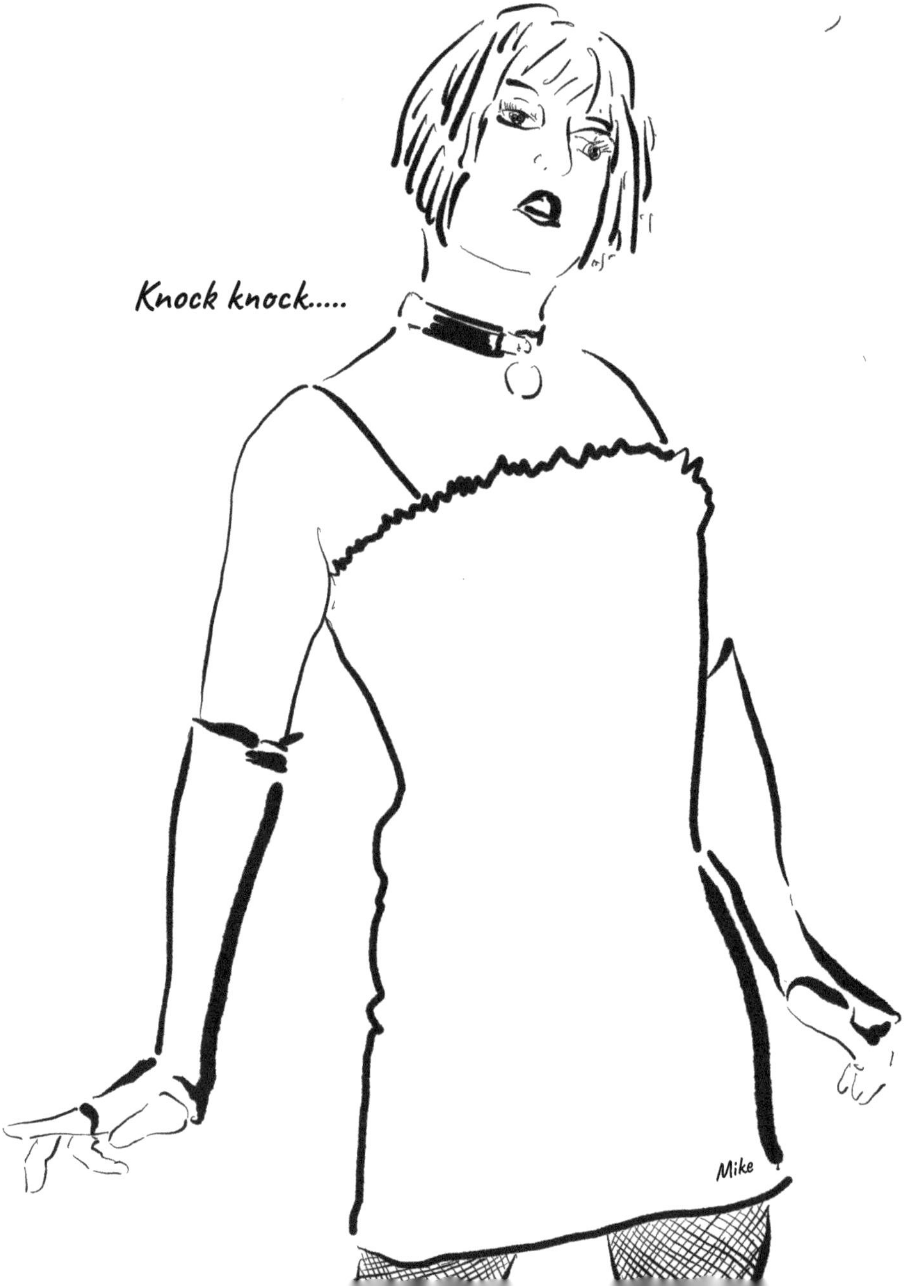

Knock knock.....

Mike

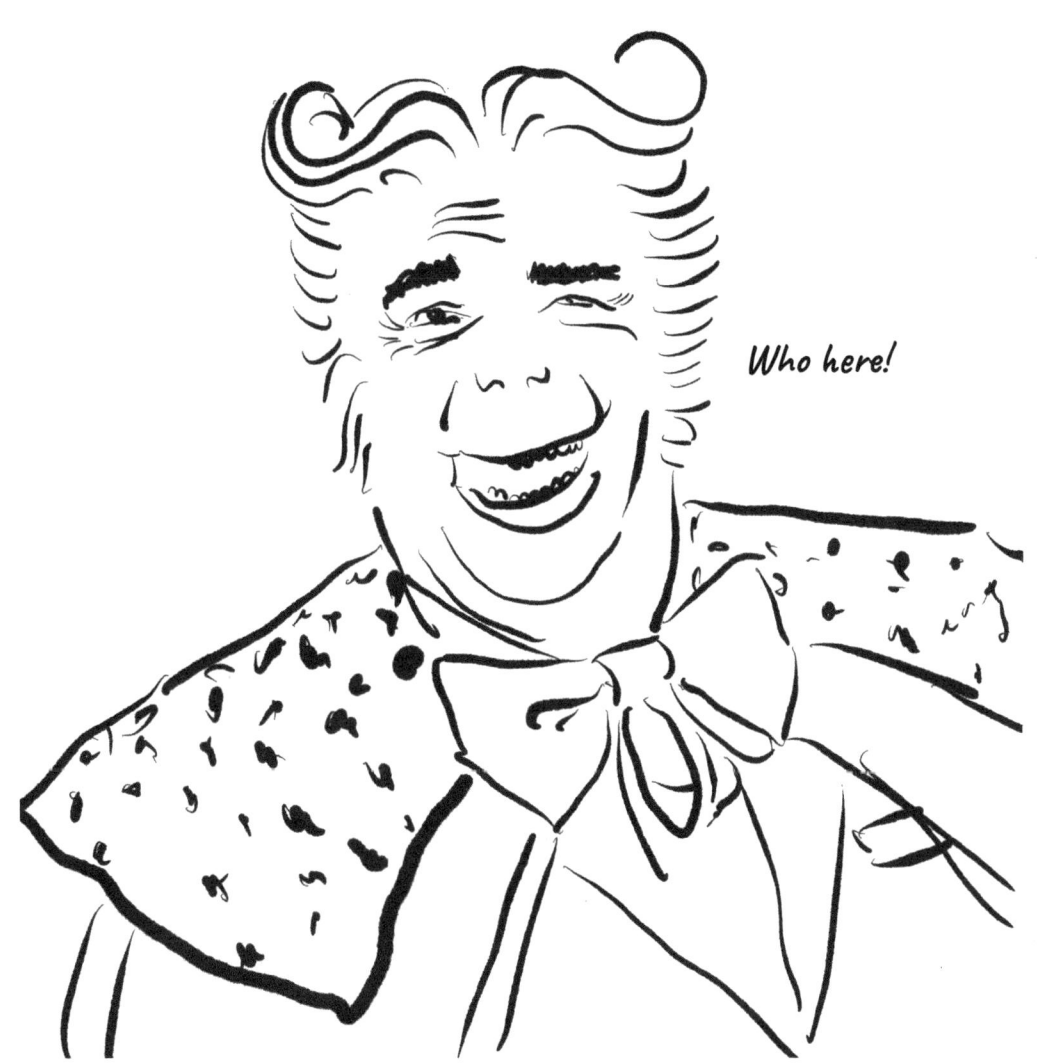

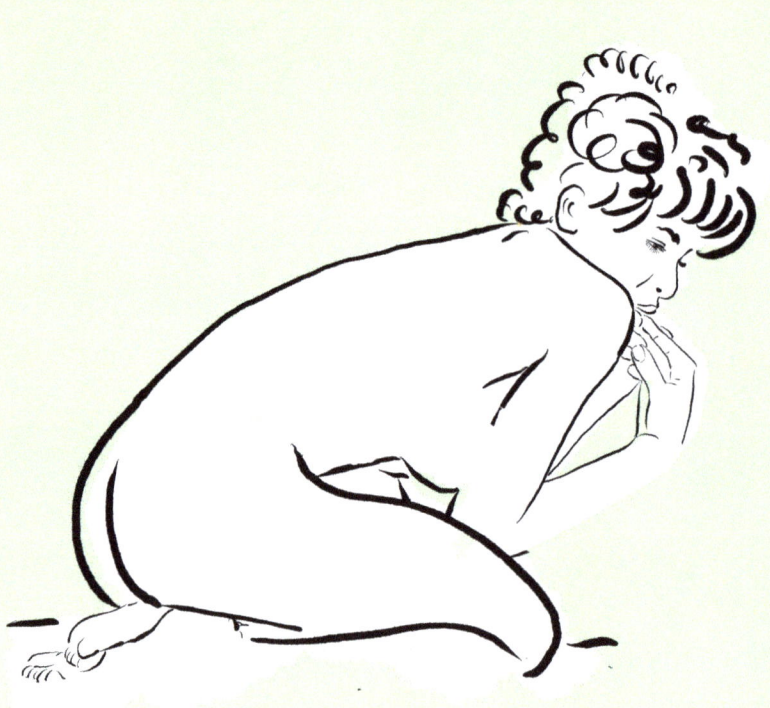

Chapter Three

Politics

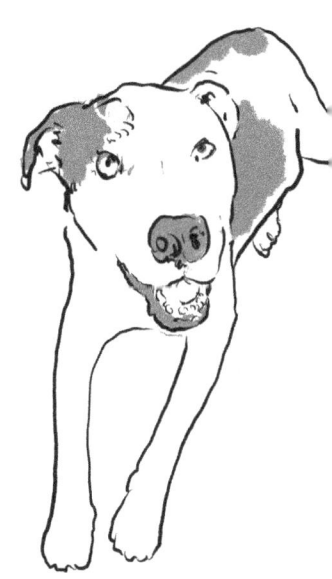

[see appendix]

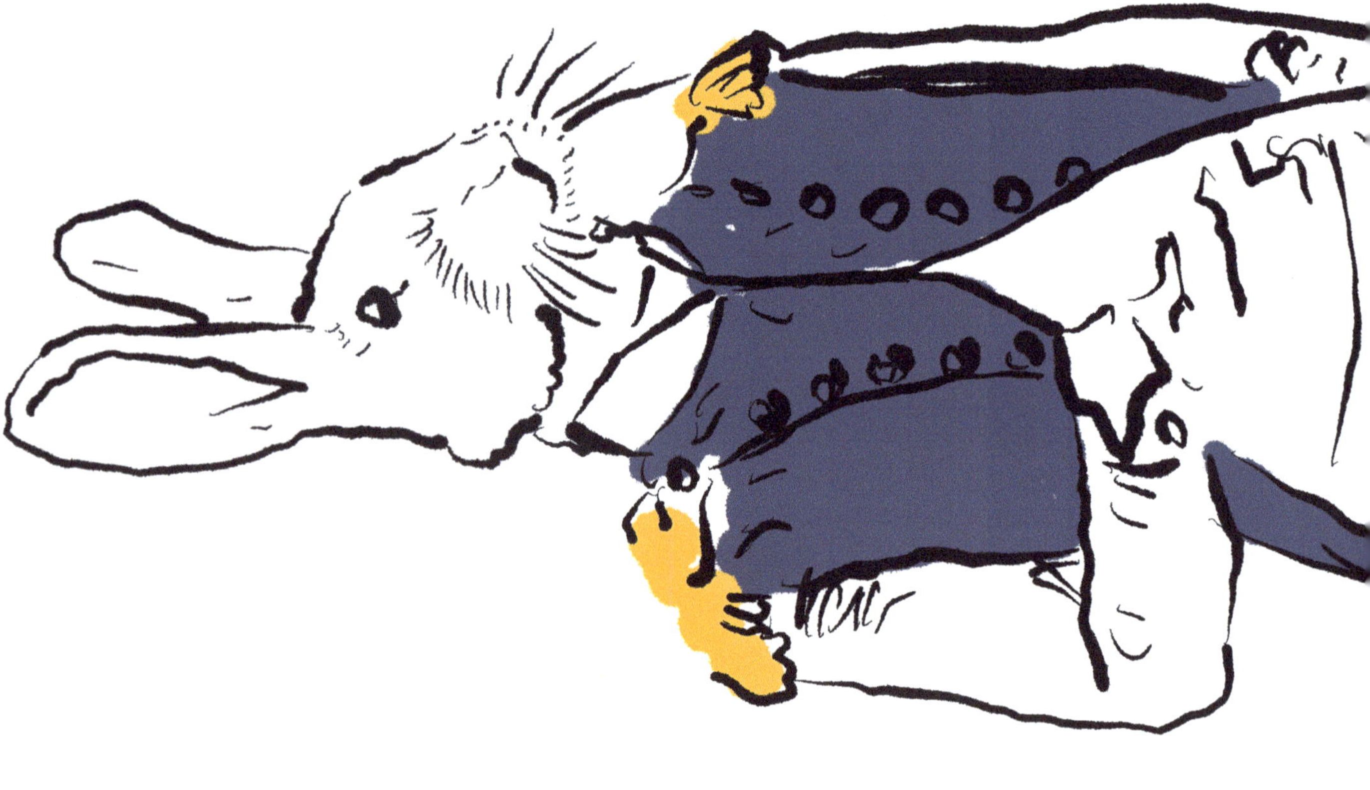

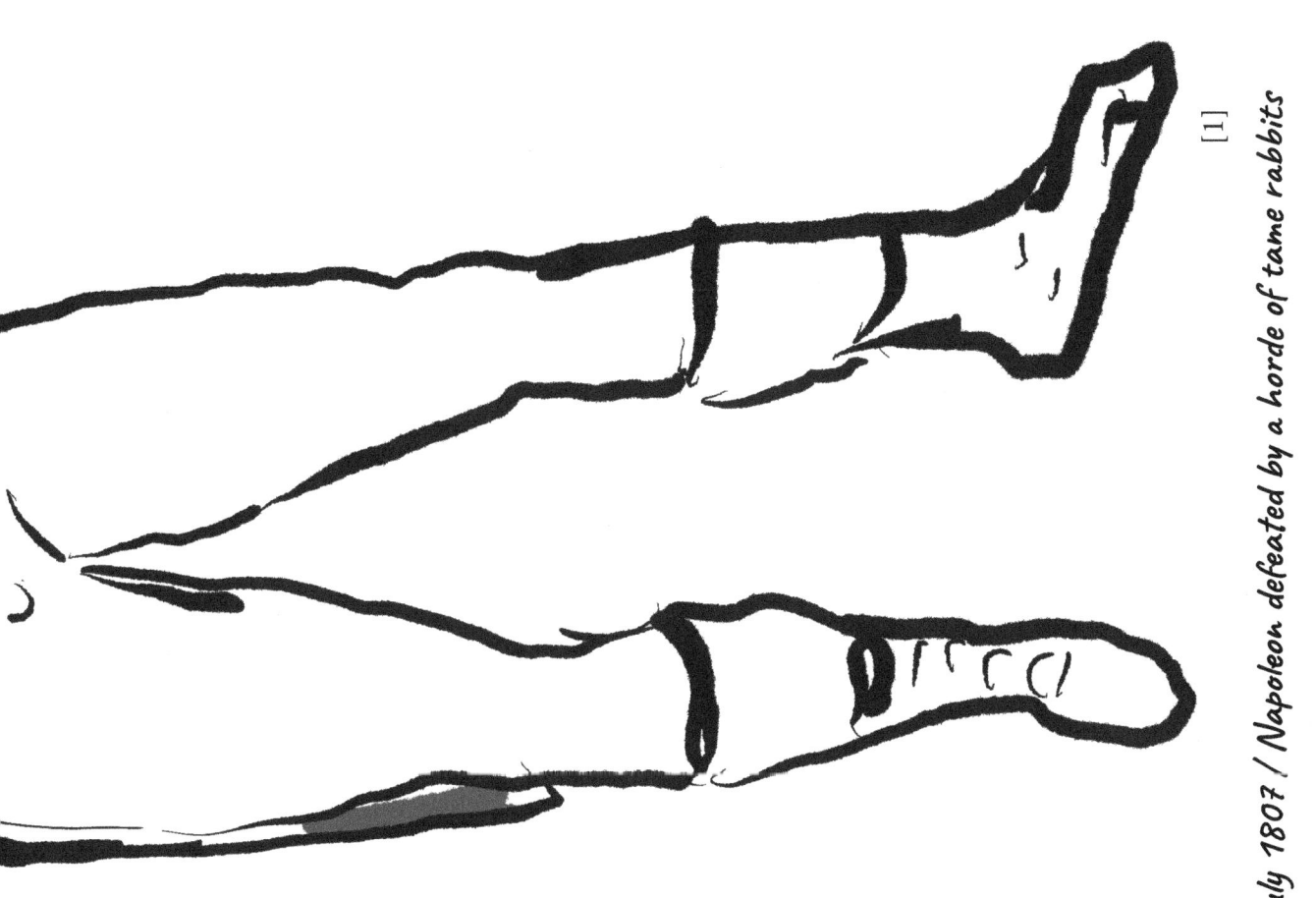

July 1807 / Napoleon defeated by a horde of tame rabbits

[1]

Black Washington on Disney +

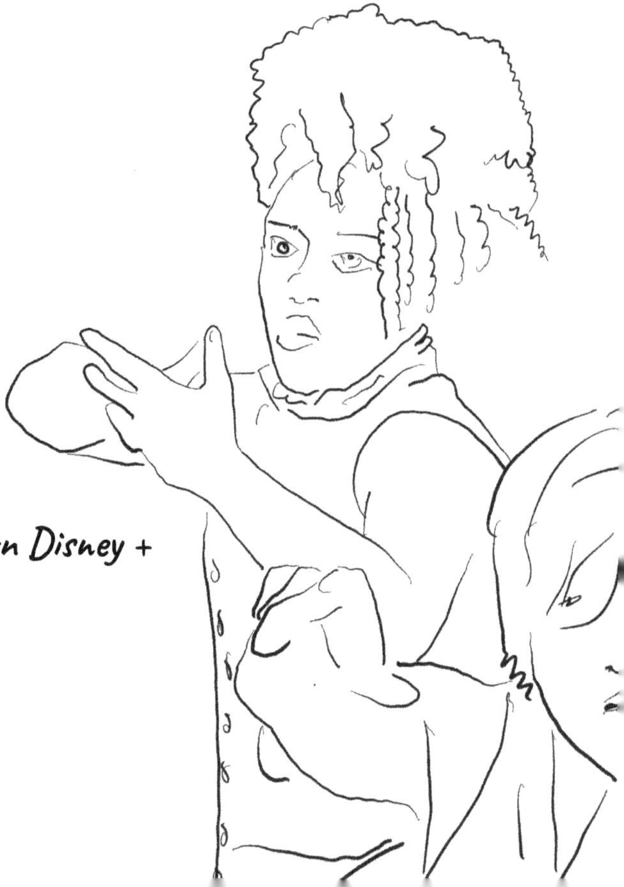

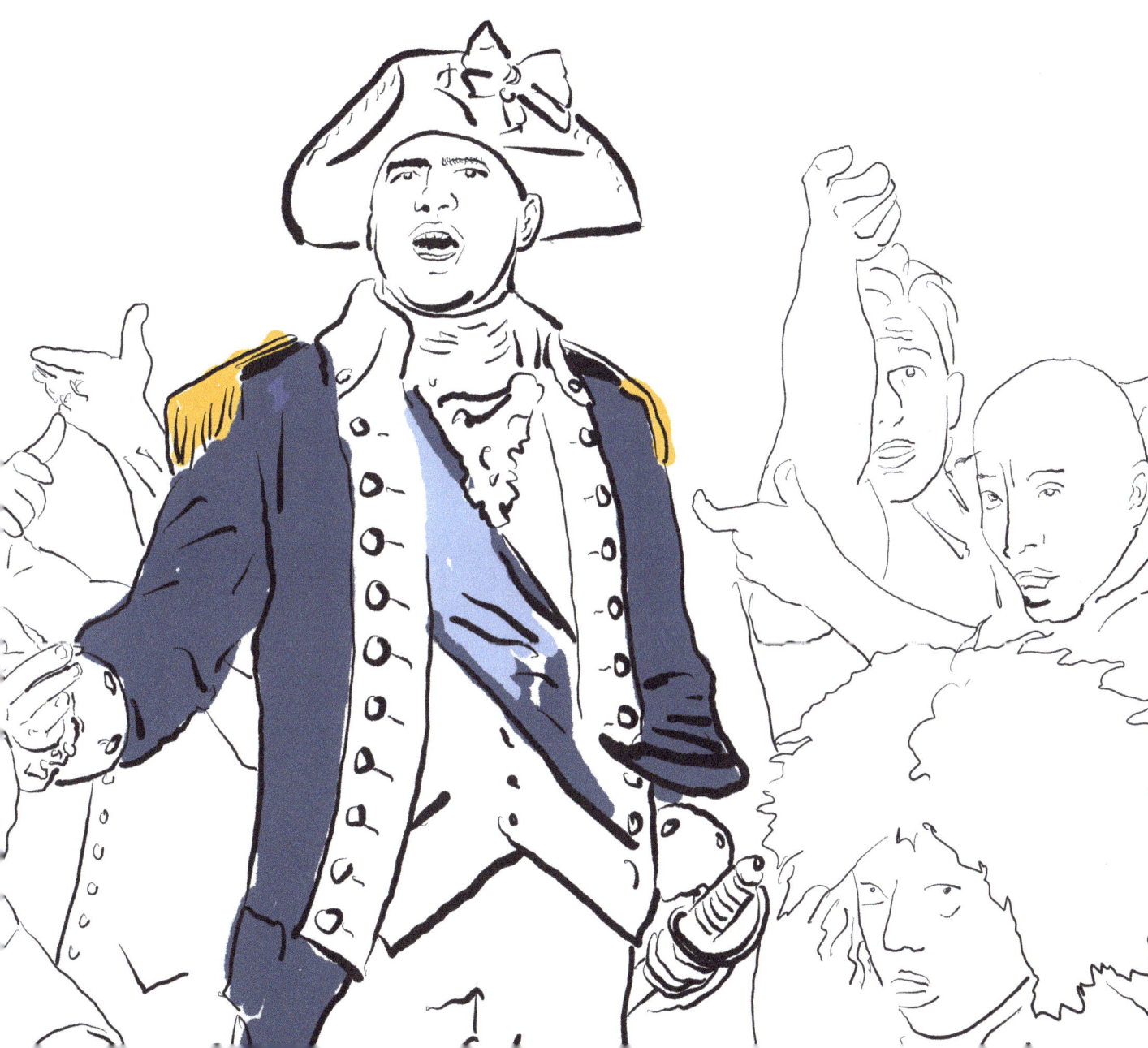

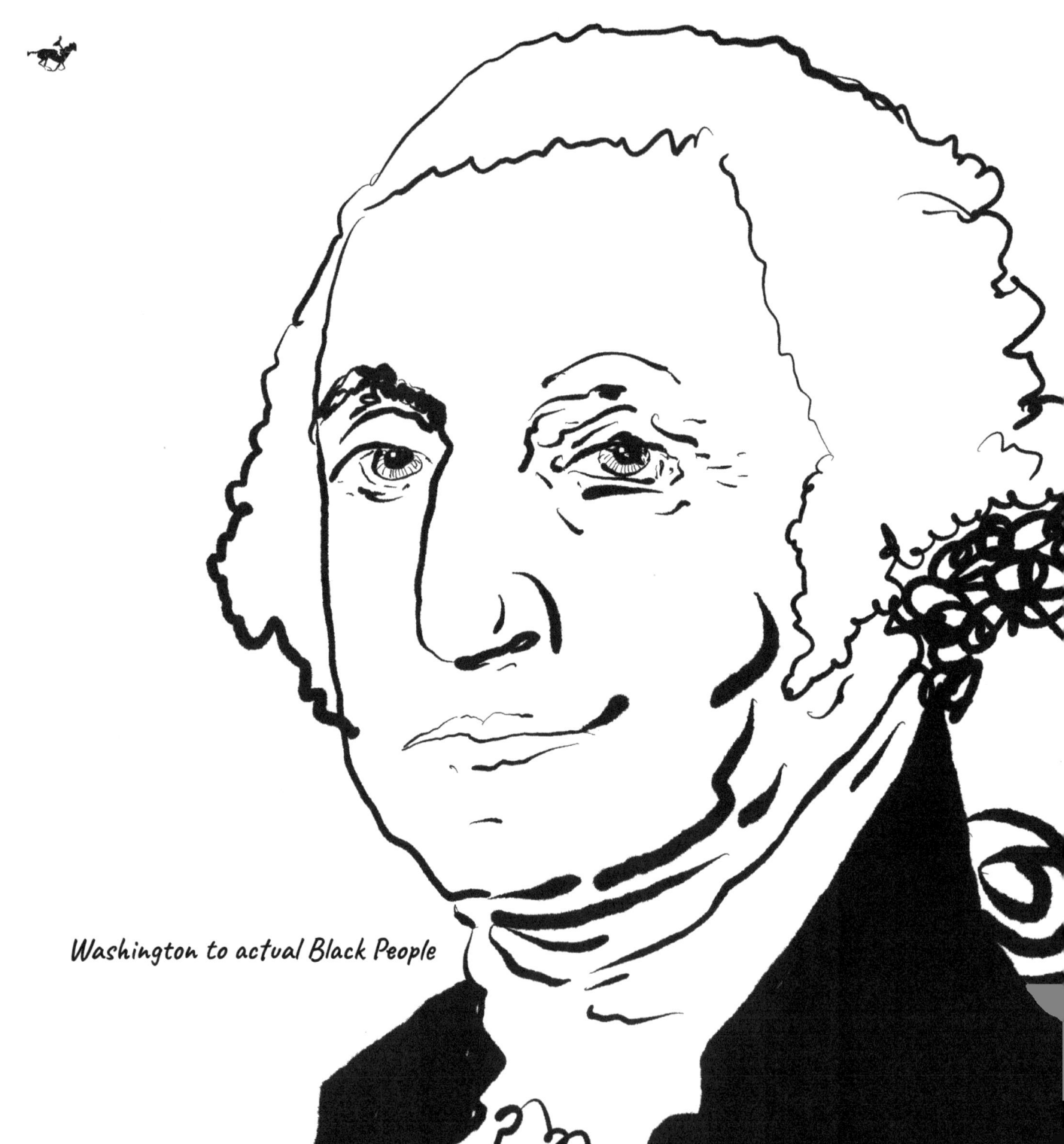

Washington to actual Black People

i like your teeth. [2]

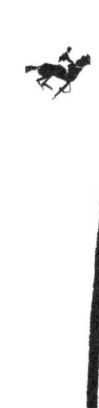

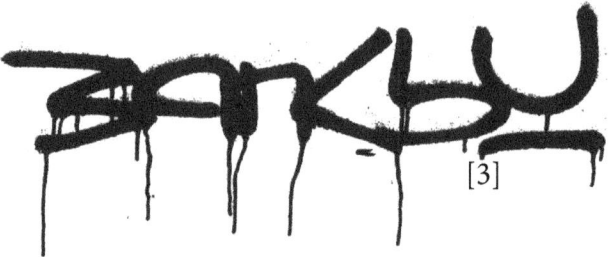

[3]

ONE POUND

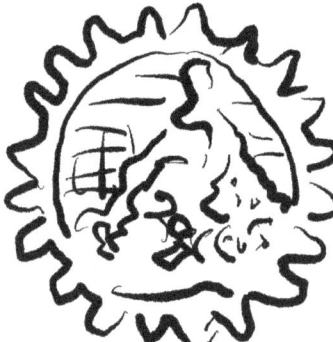

LONDON
FOR THE POUND

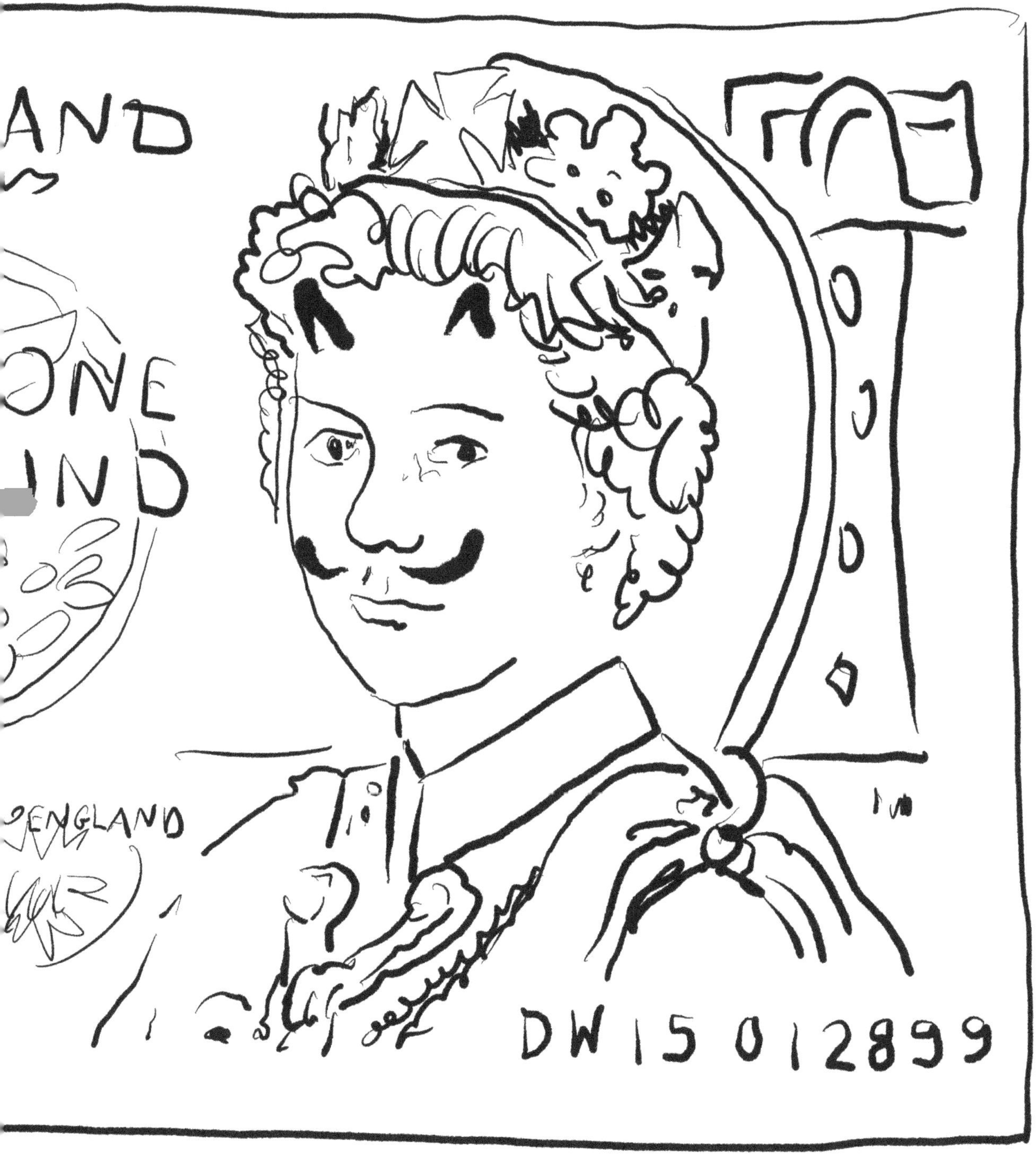

AND
ONE
IND
ENGLAND
DW15 012899

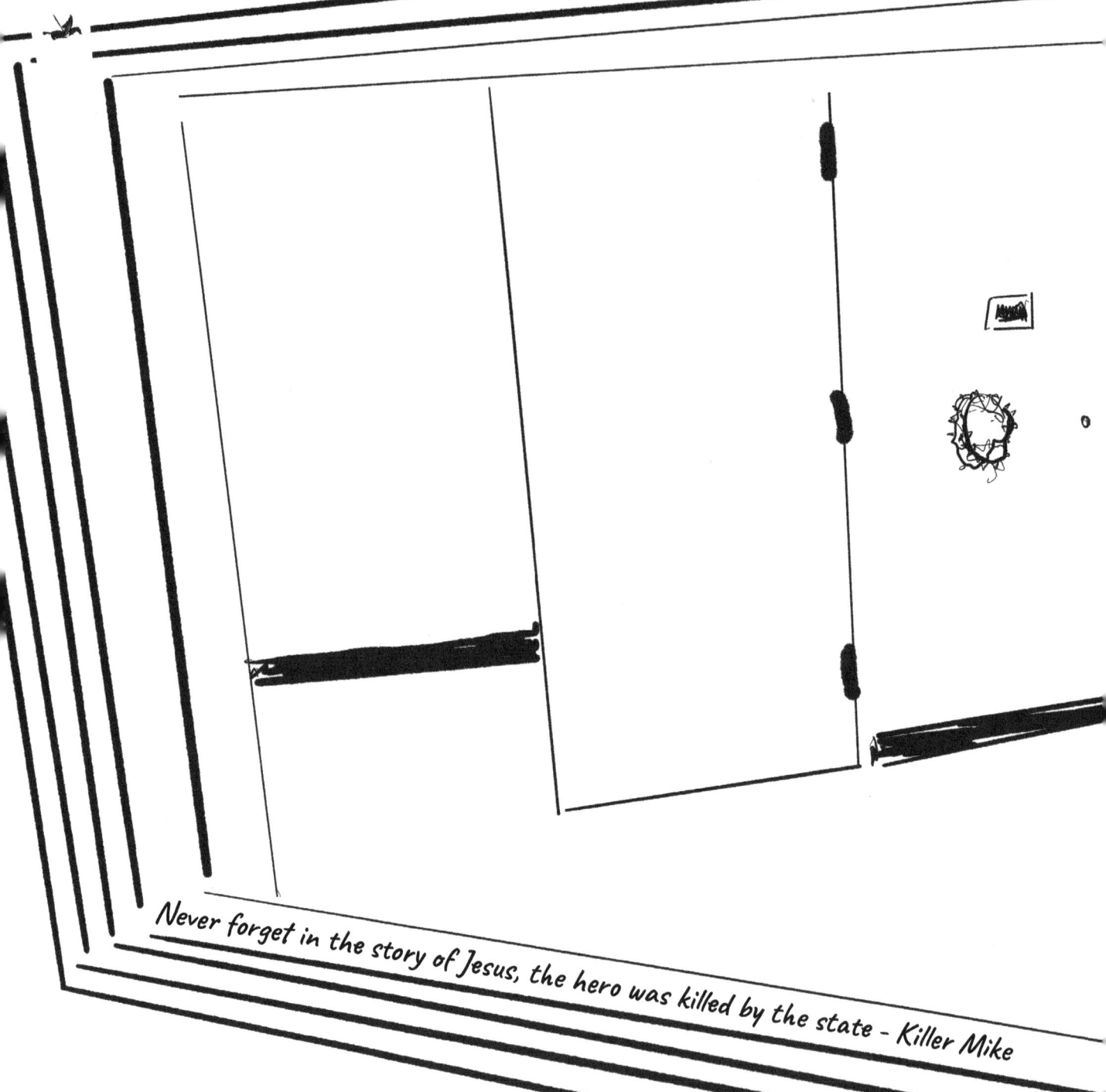

Never forget in the story of Jesus, the hero was killed by the state - Killer Mike

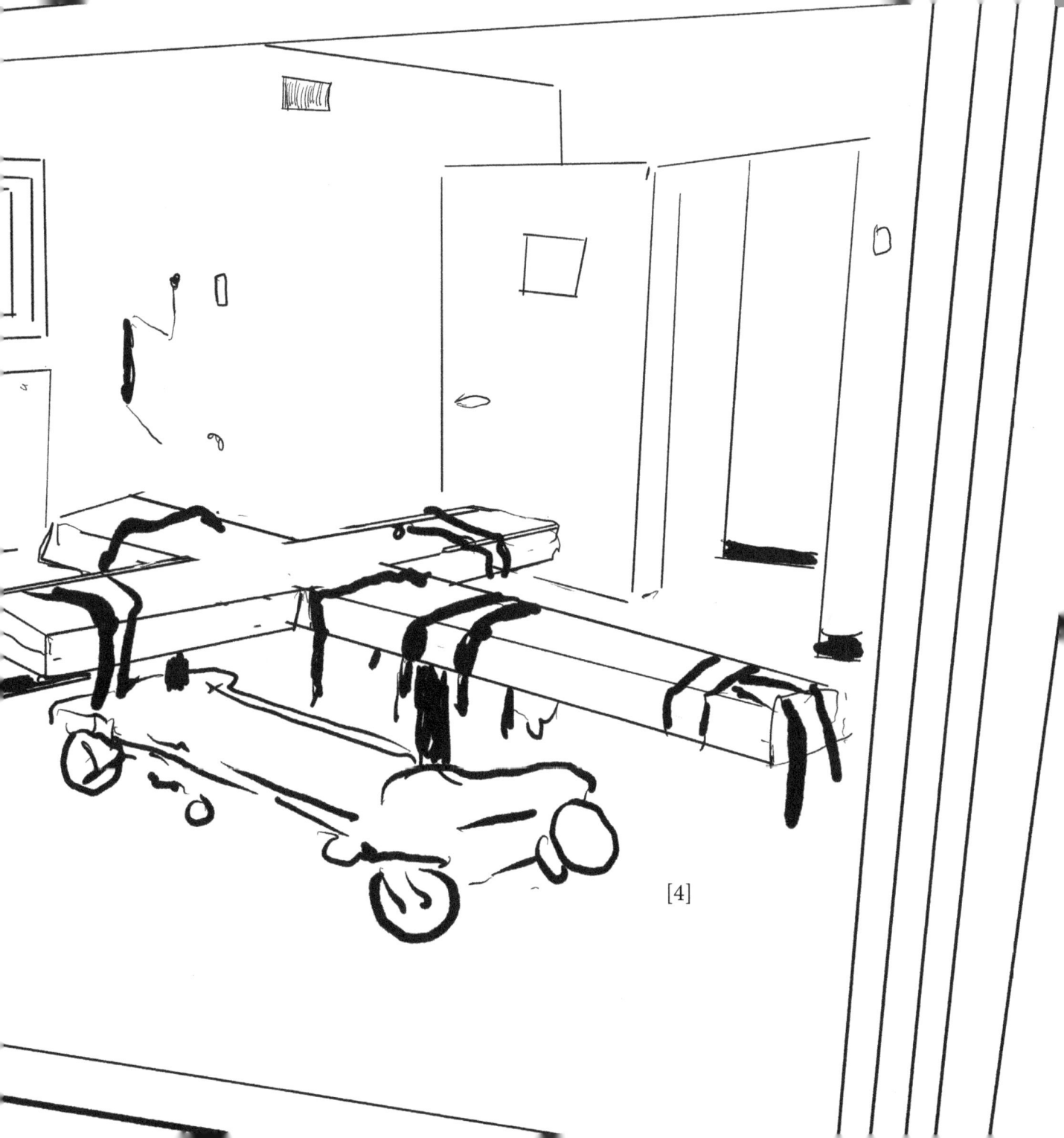

[4]

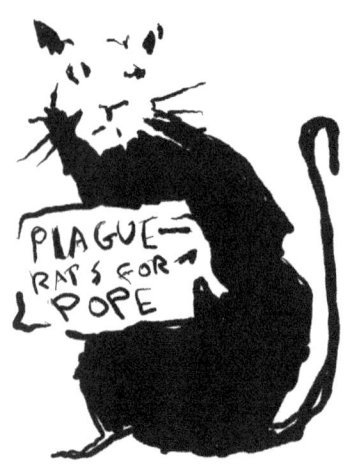

[5]

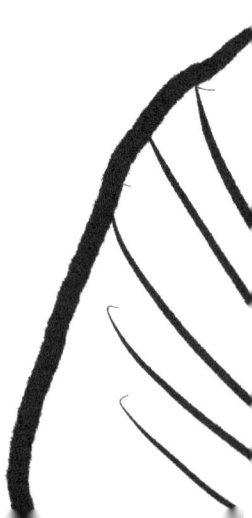

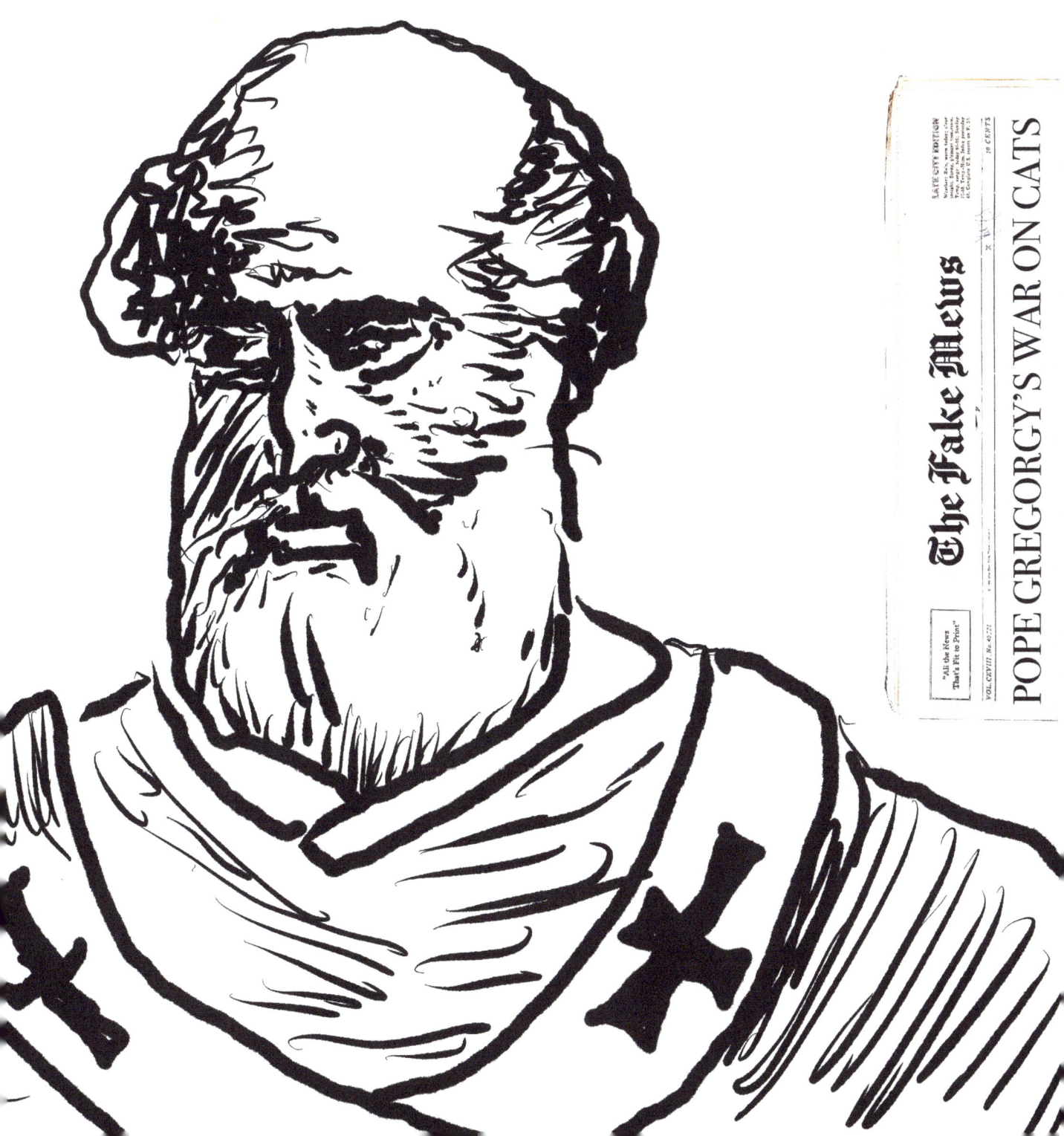

The Fake Mews

LATE CITY EDITION

"All the News That's Fit to Print"

VOL. CXVIII. No. 40,721

10 CENTS

POPE GREGORGY'S WAR ON CATS

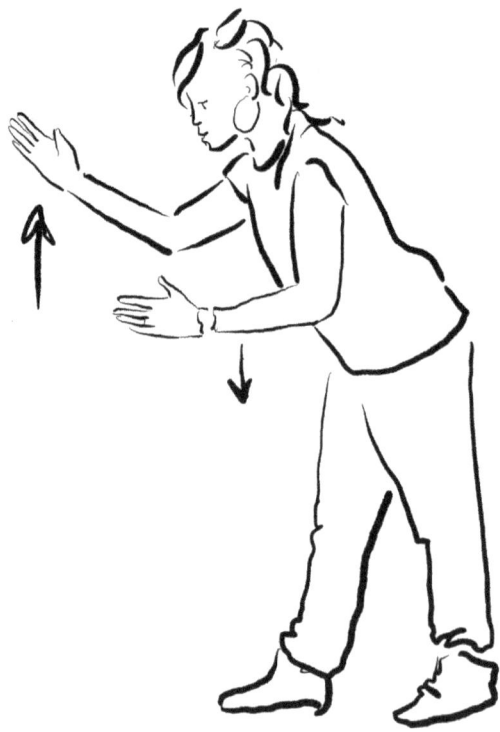

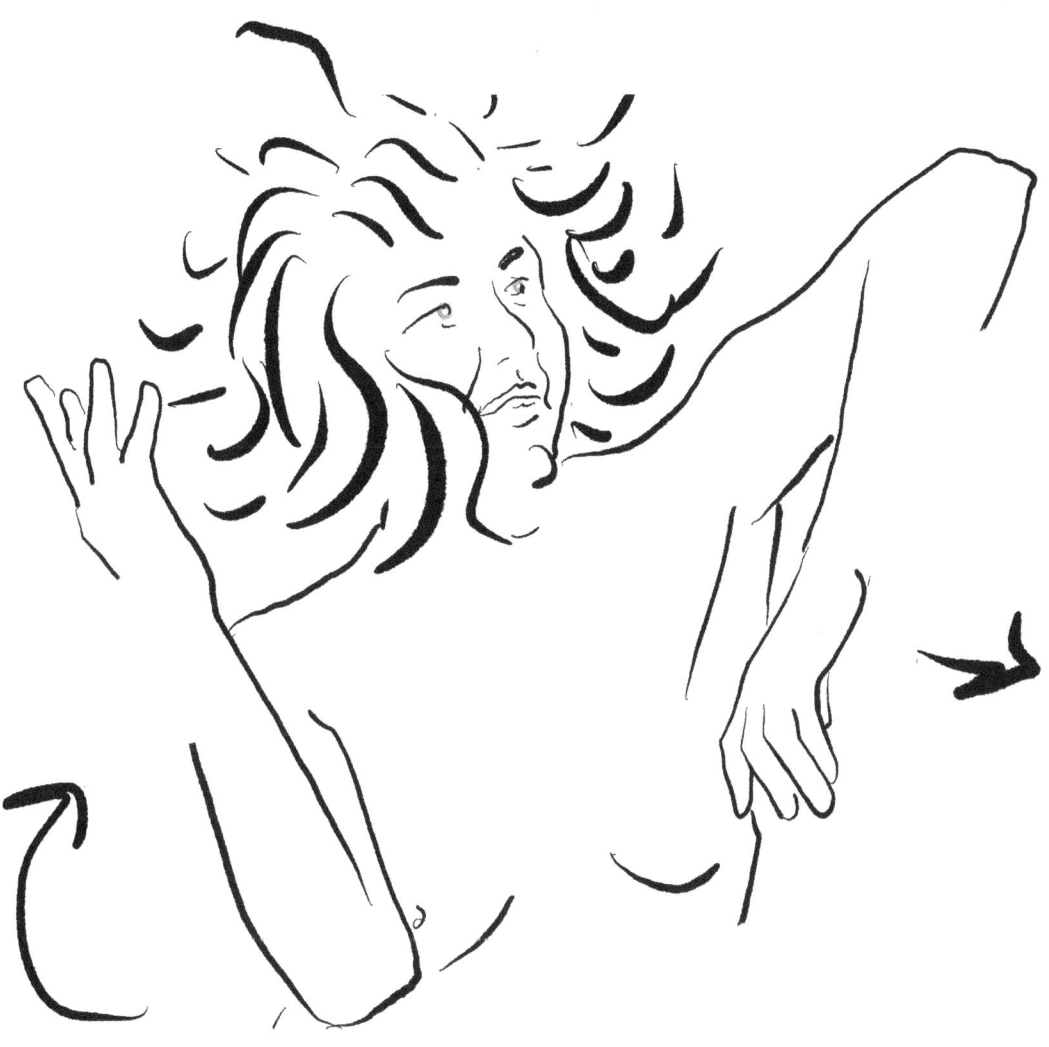

[6]
Technical Americans don't dance like this

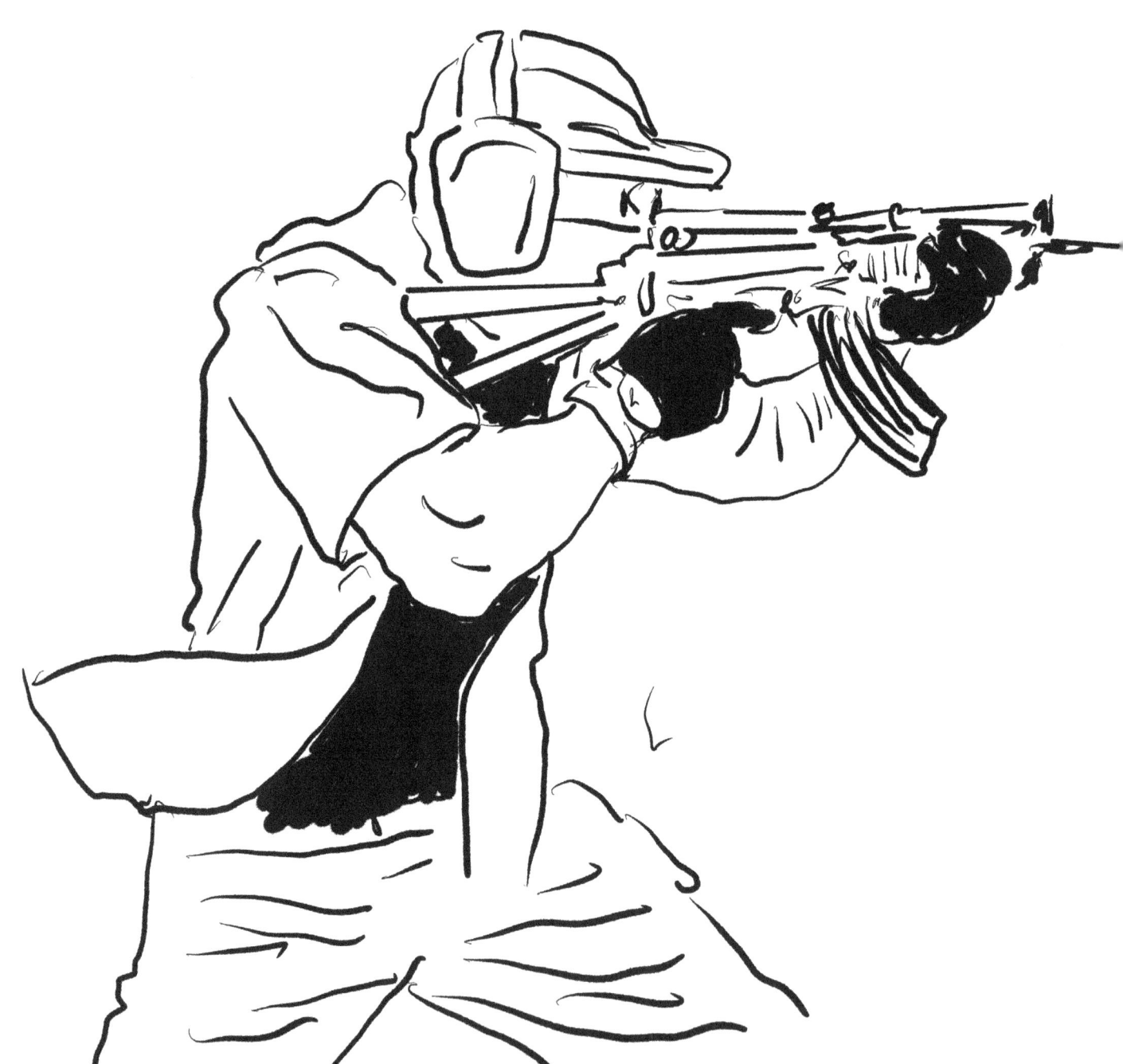

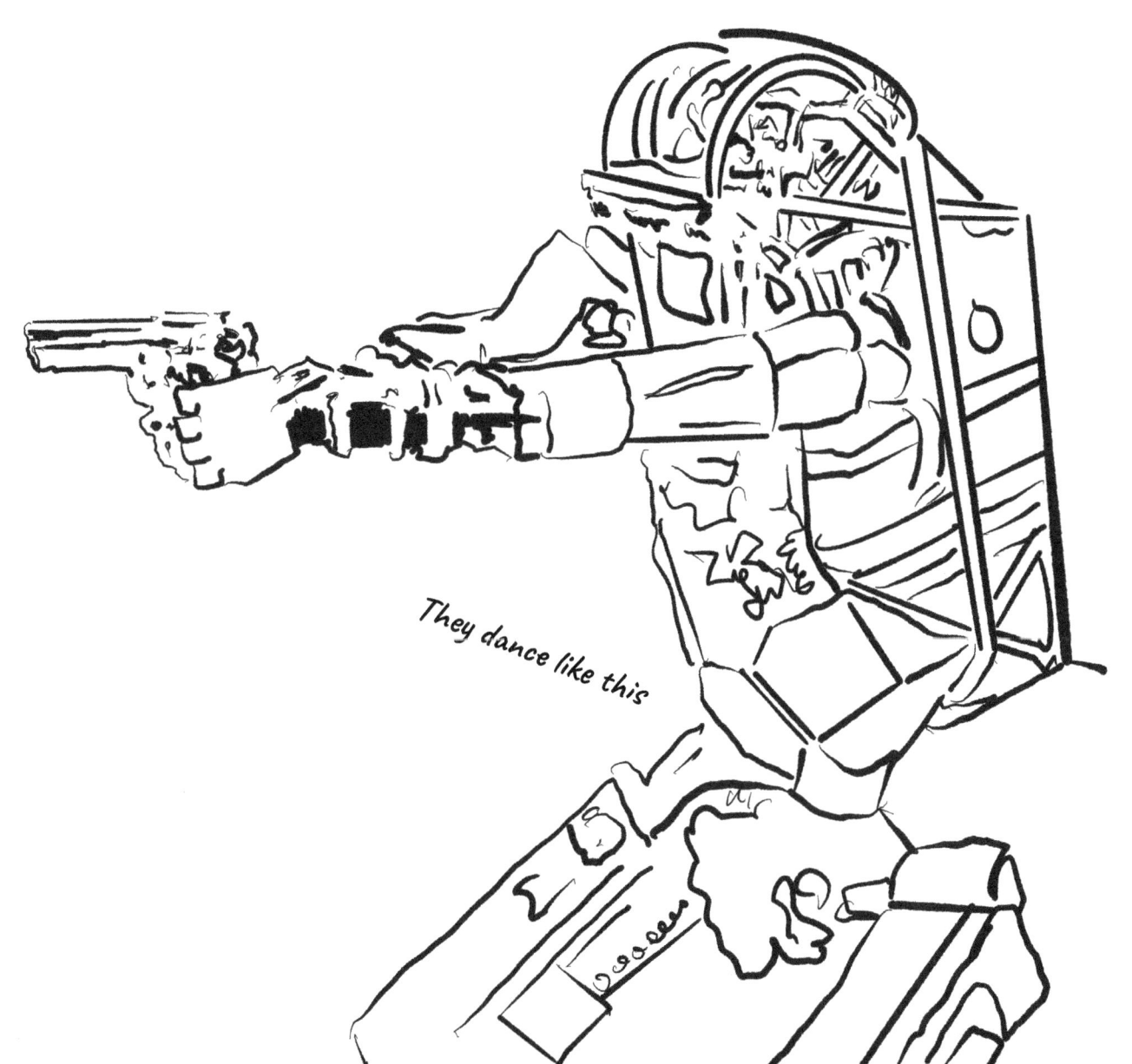

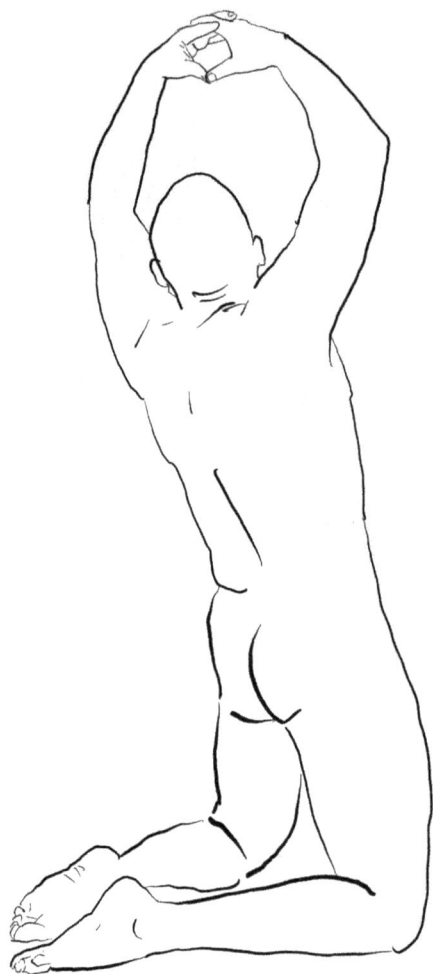

Chapter Four

An Elegant Rendition of the Spins

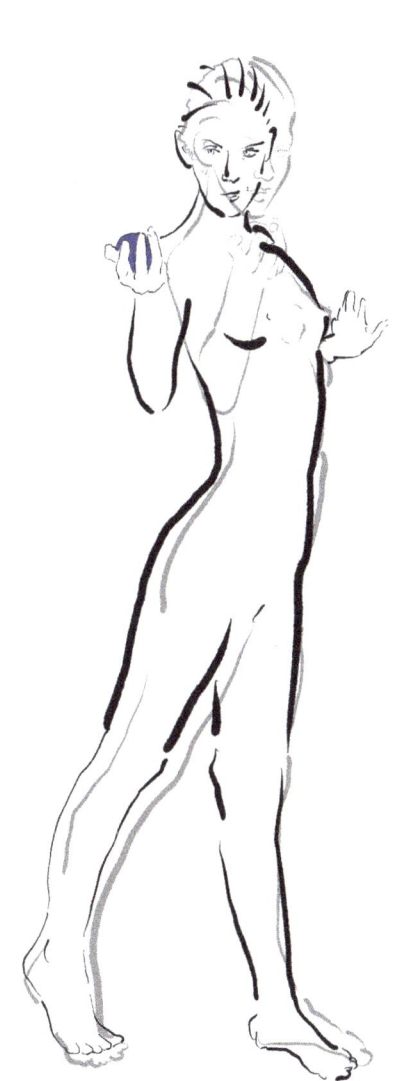

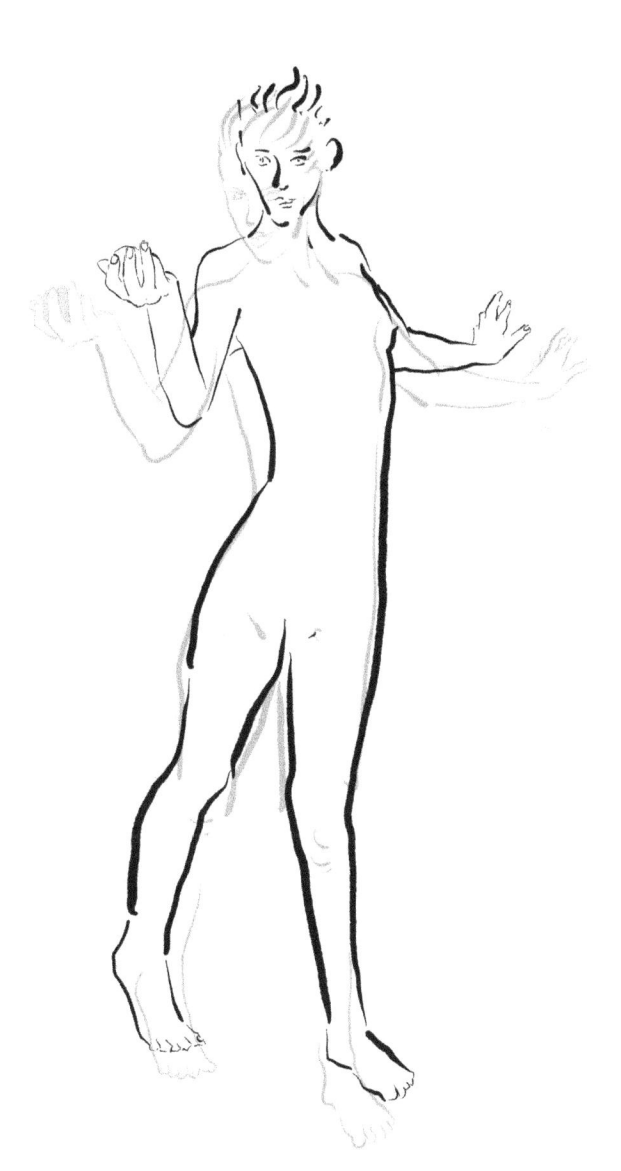

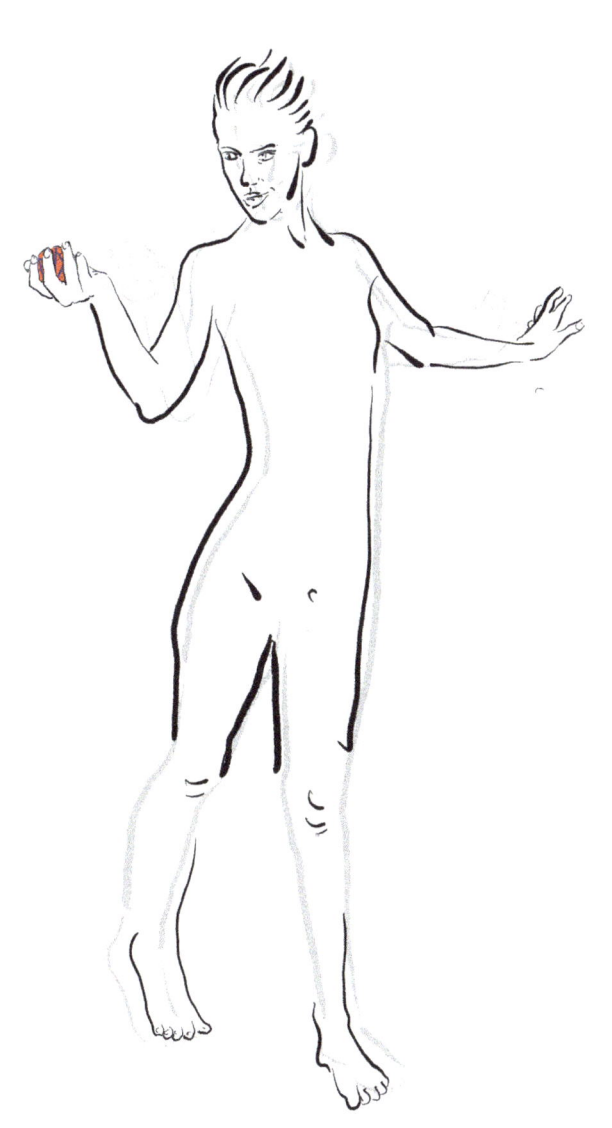

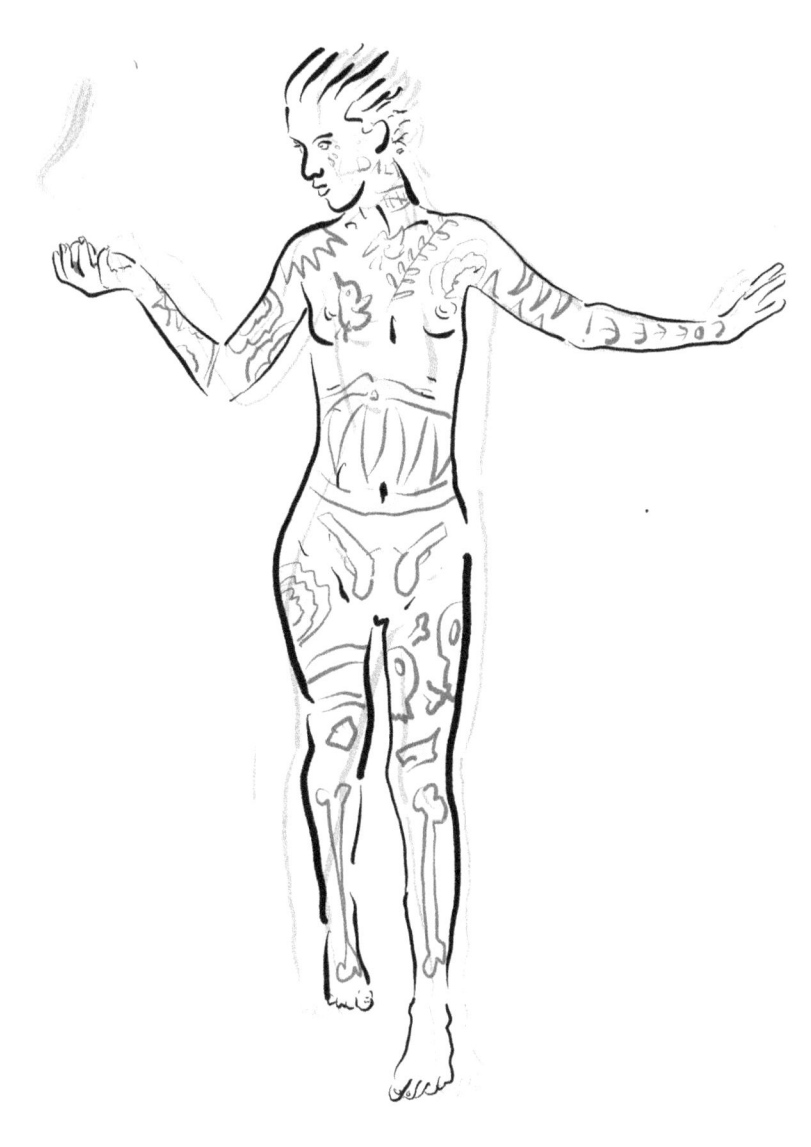

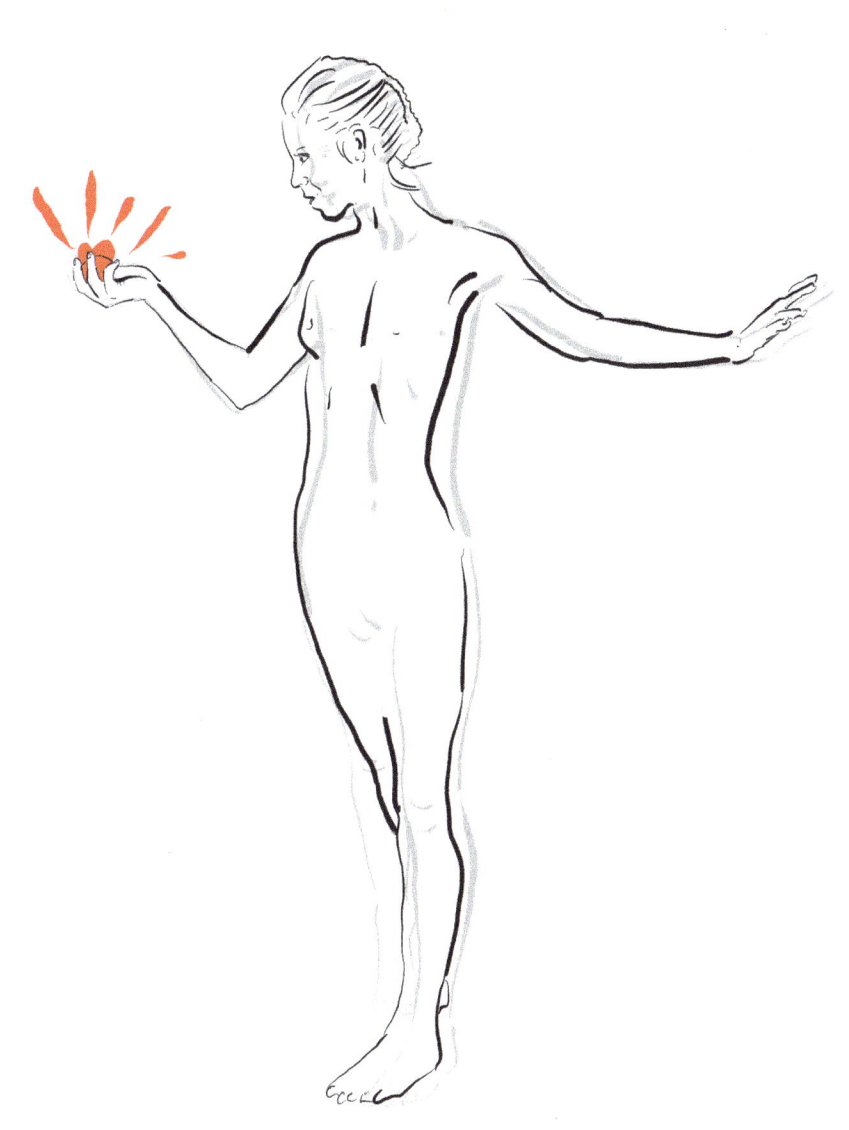

श

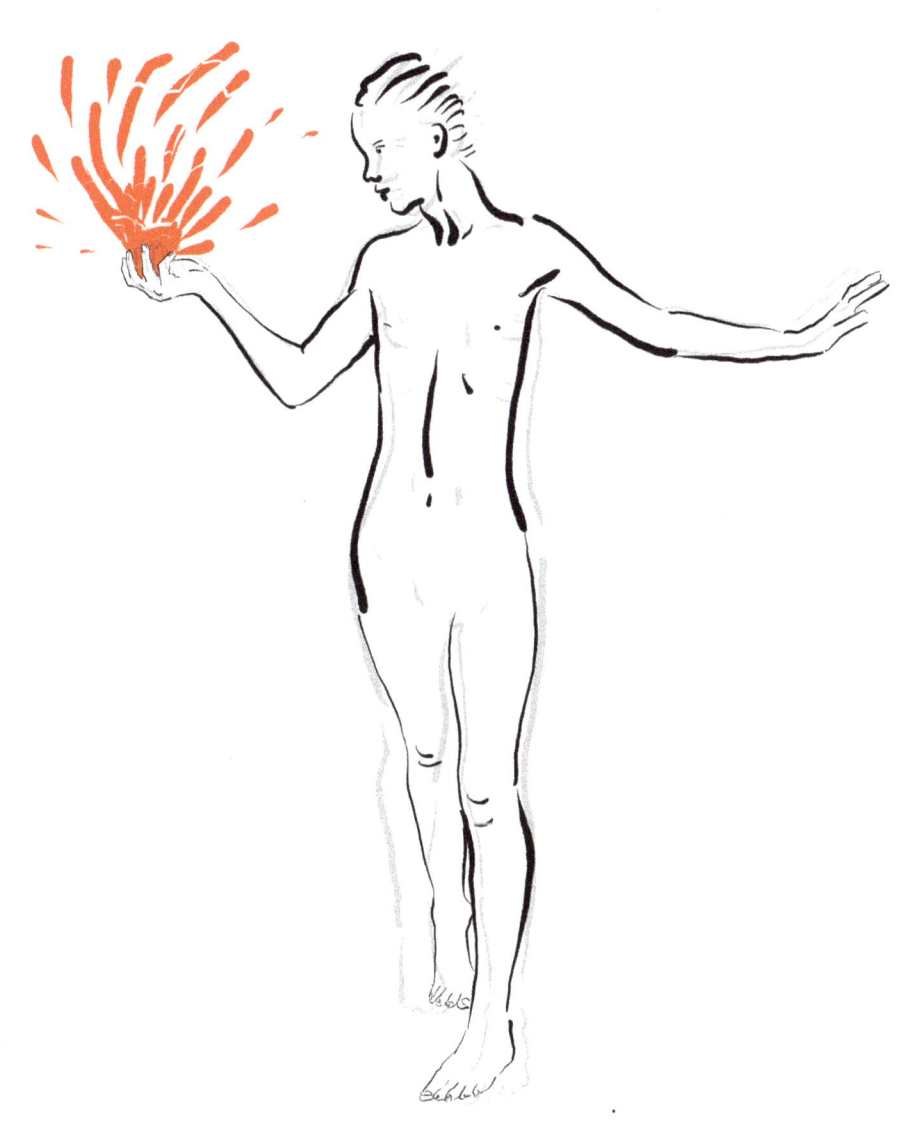

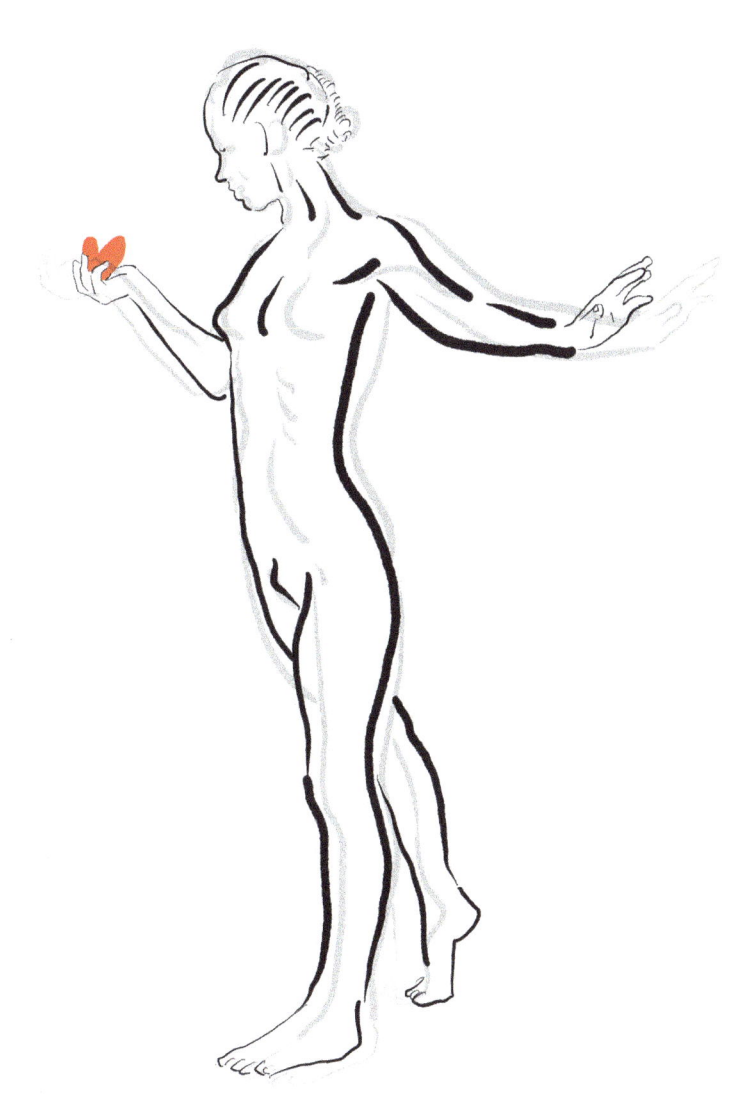

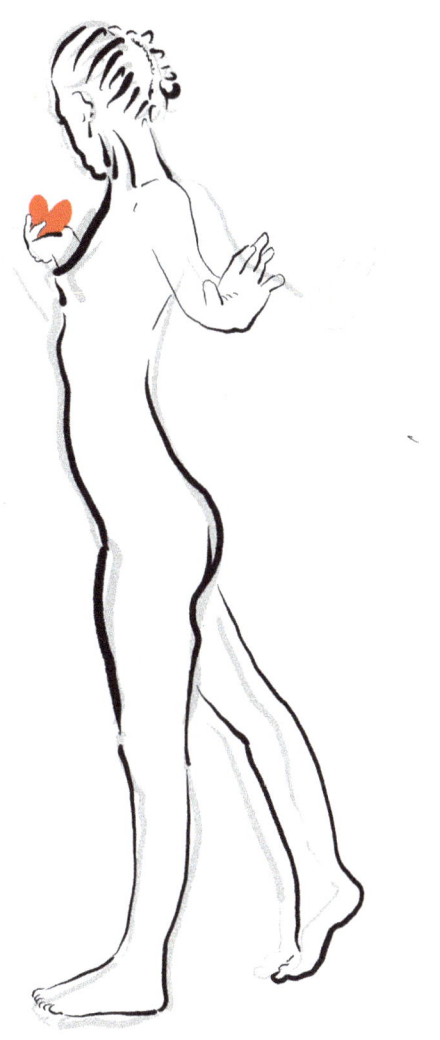

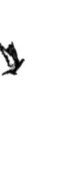

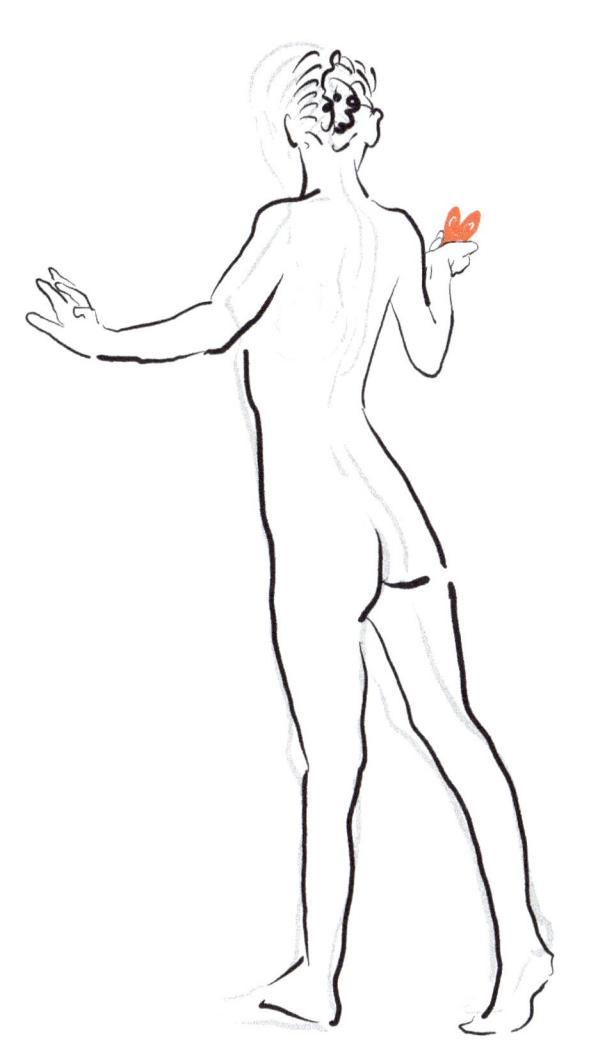

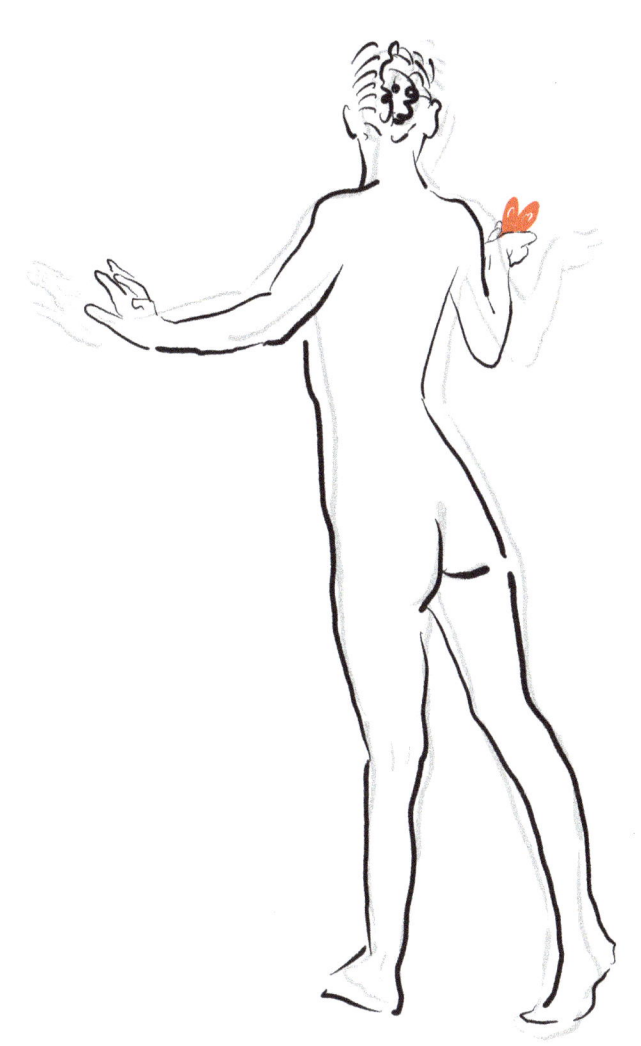

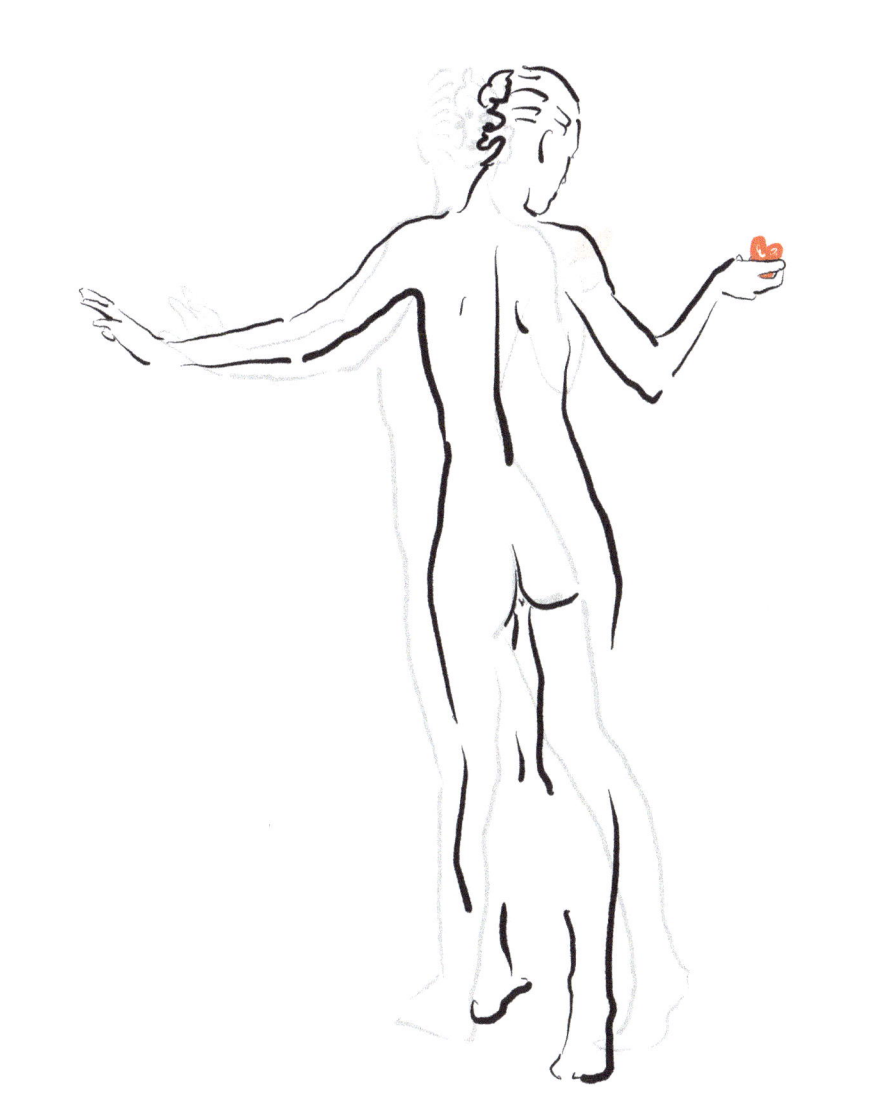

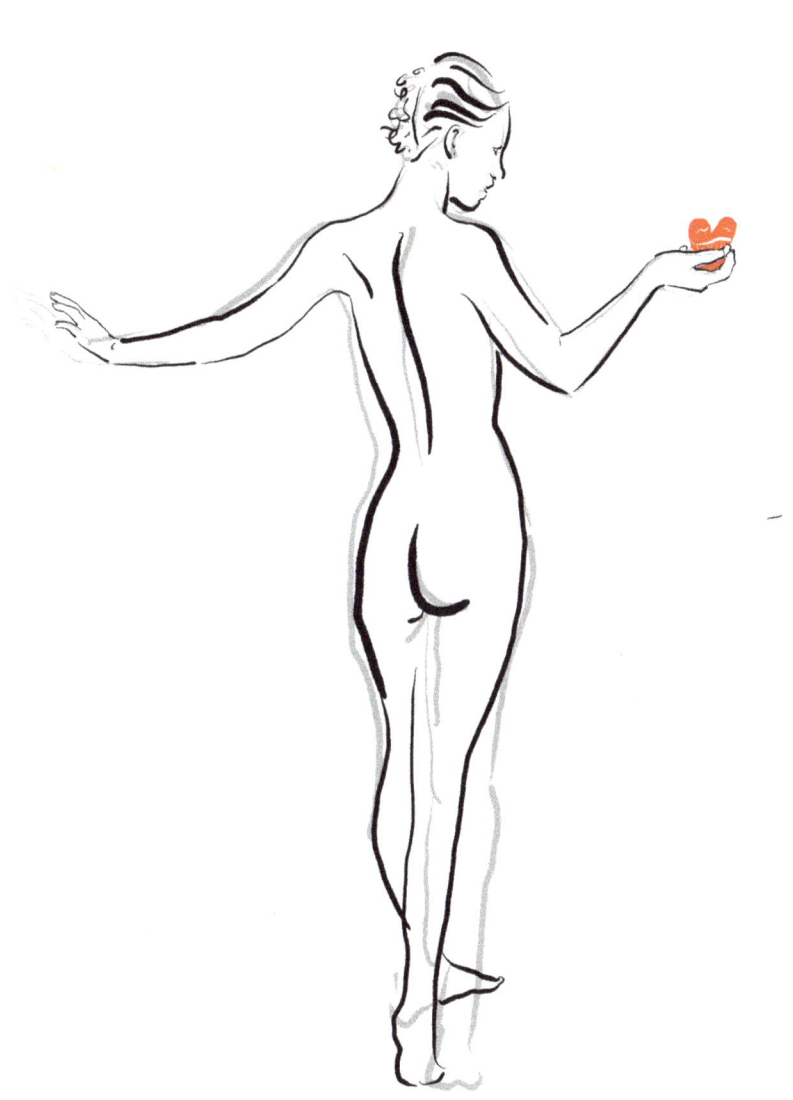

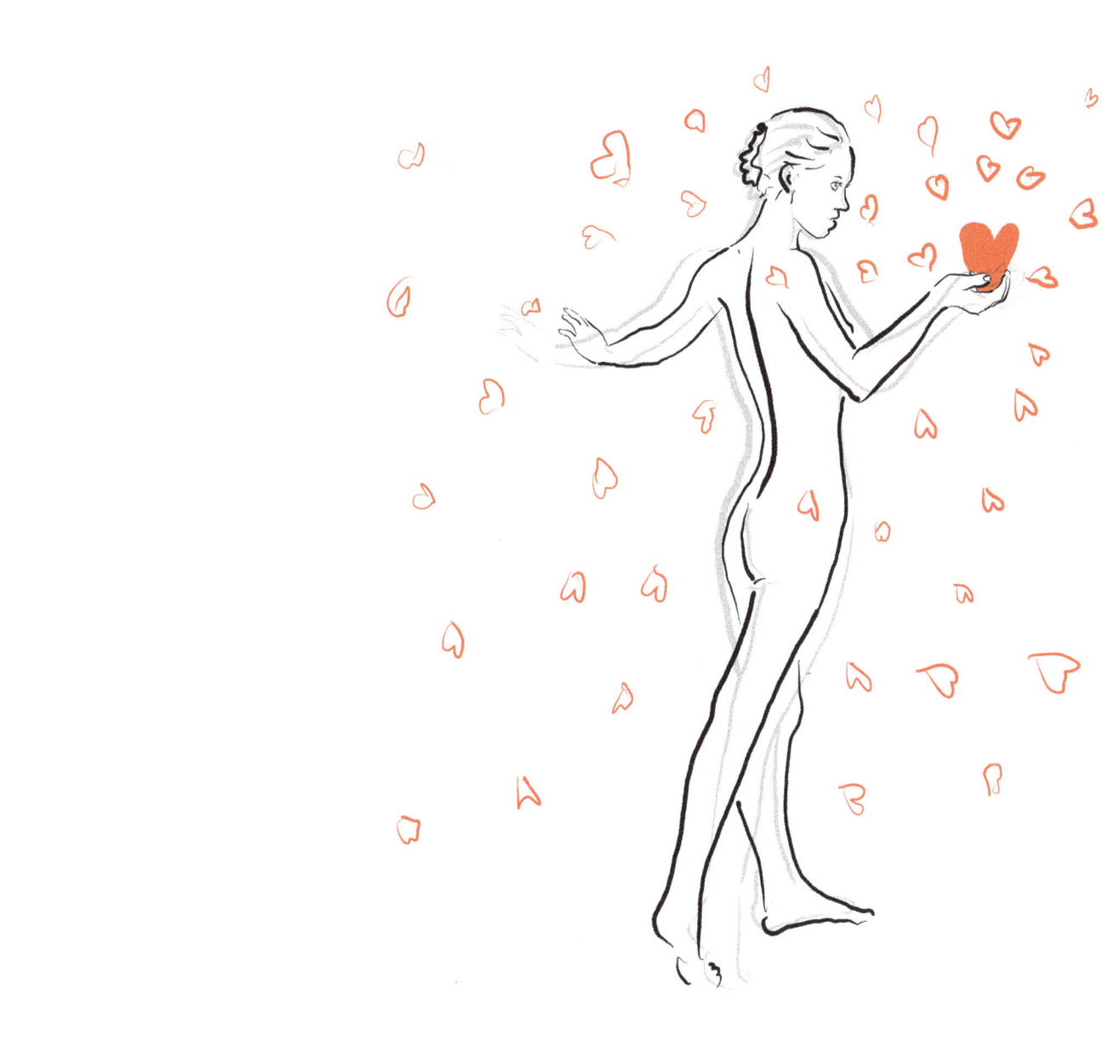

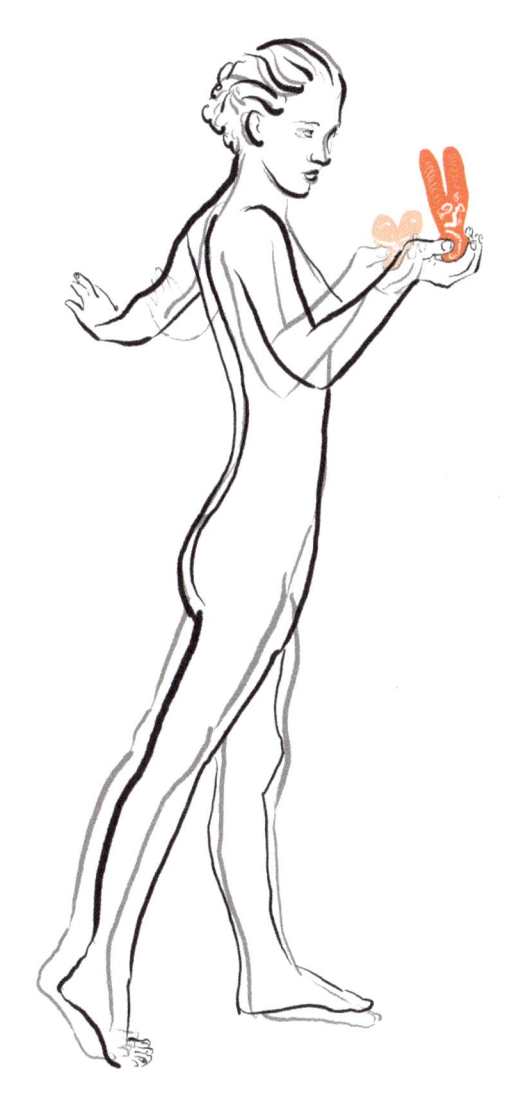

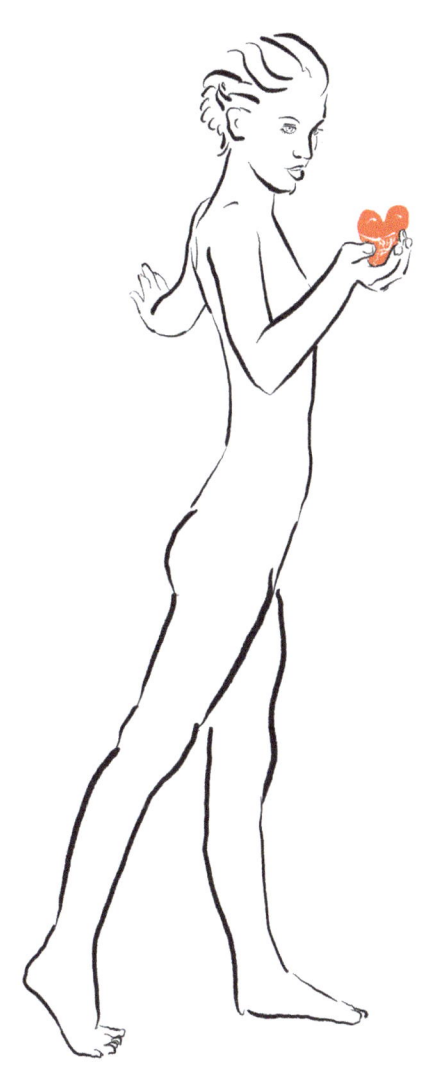

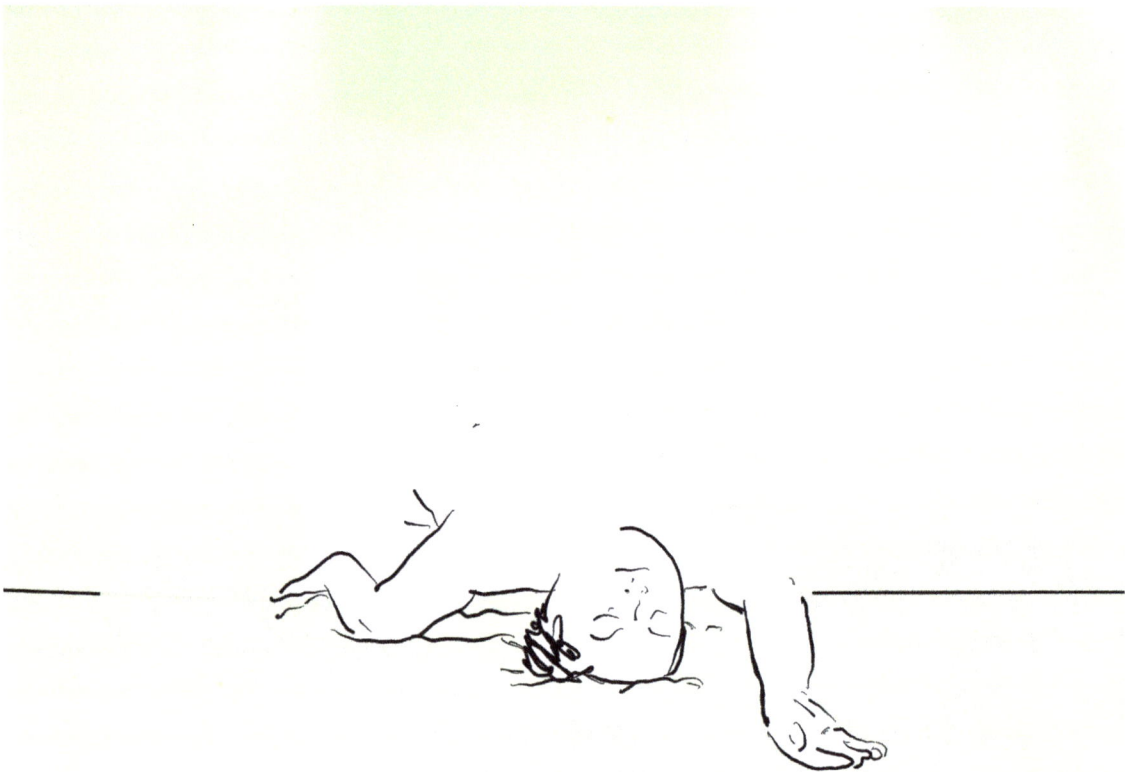

Chapter Five

A Final Thought

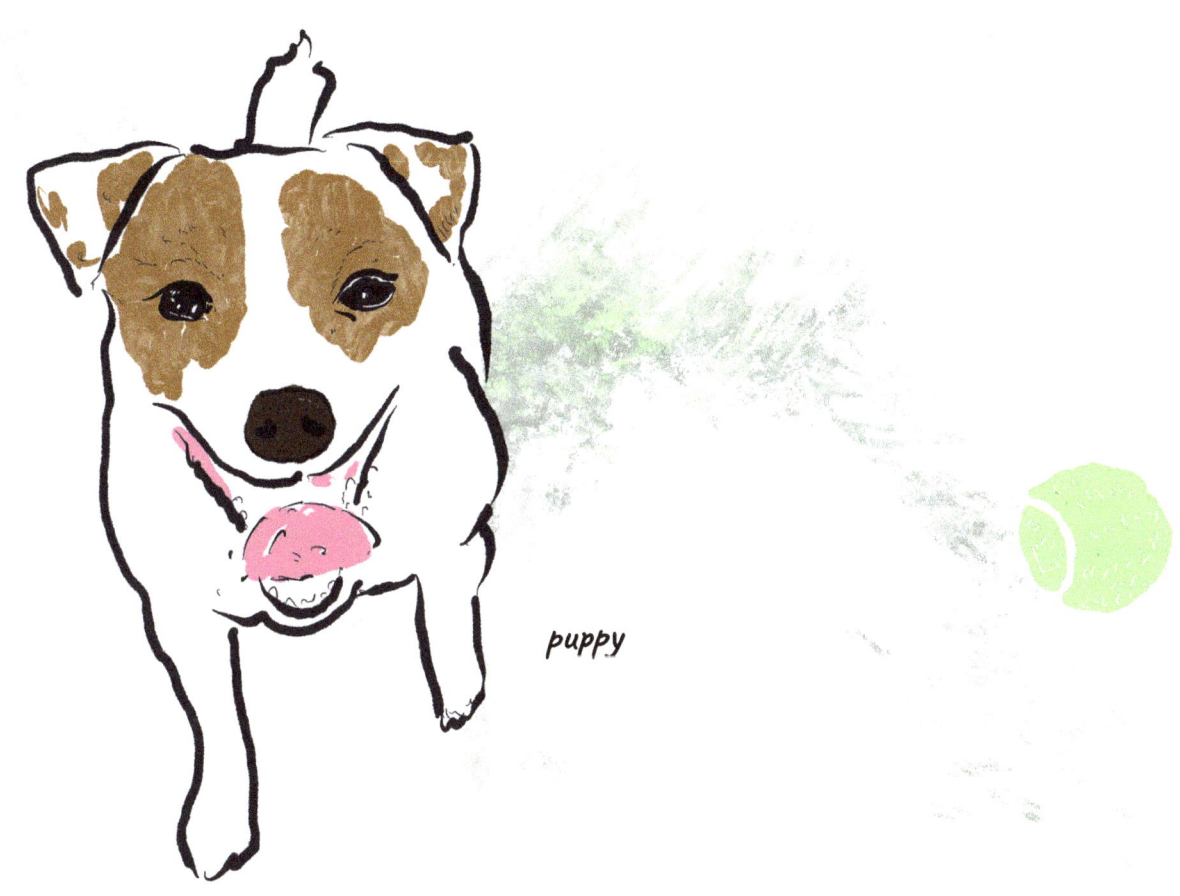

puppy

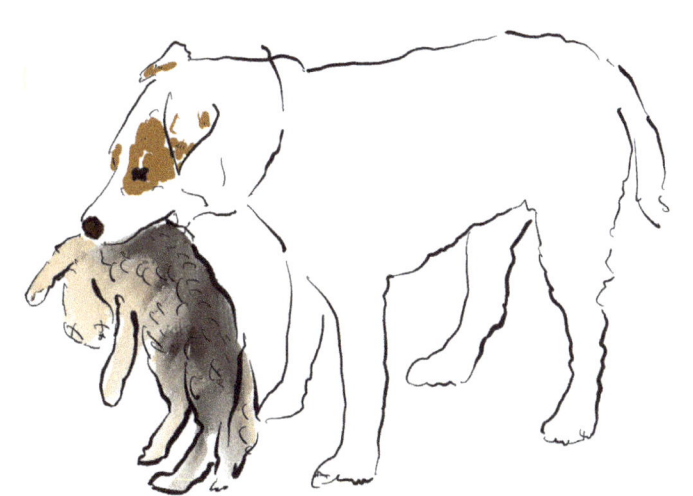

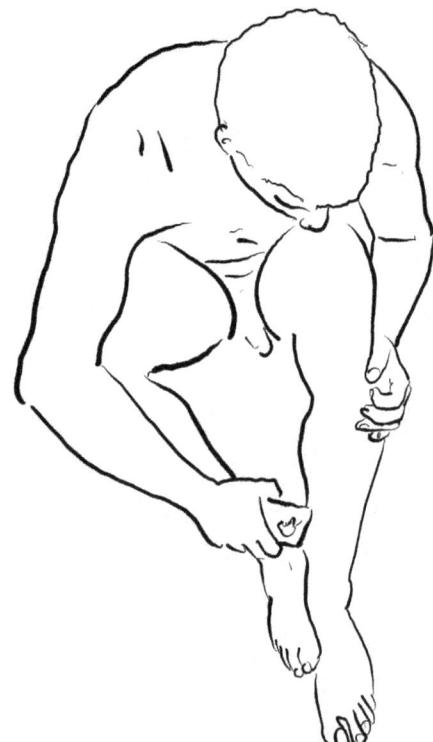

Appendix

Davis said I should explain the Politics Chapter

1: In July 1807 Napoleon signed the Treaties of Tilsit and wanted to party.

His Chief of Staff Alexandre Berthier made it happen.

Berthier invited military bigwigs and sourced a slew of rabbits. The men caged them all along the edges of a clearing. When Napoleon, with guns, started the hunt, the rabbits were released from their cages. And so began the hunt!

A strange thing happened, the bunnies instead of running scared, turned on him. The rabbits swarmed his legs and climbed up his jacket. Napoleon tried shooing them and chasing them. But it kept coming. Napoleon retreated, fleeing to his carriage. The flood of bunnies continued—some reportedly leapt into the carriage. The attack ceased only as the coach rolled away. The man who was dominating Europe was no match for a battle with bunnies.

It was Berthier's fault. Rather than trapping wild hares, his men had bought tame rabbits from local farmers. As a result, the rabbits didn't see Napoleon as a fearsome hunter. They saw him as a waiter bringing out the day's food. To them, the emperor was effectively a giant head of lettuce.

Abridged Version of Lucas Reilly's viral article "The Time Napoleon Was Attacked by Rabbits. "

2. George Washington's Mount Vernon estate says it will no longer sell a souvenir depicting the founding father's false teeth amid criticism that Washington's dentures were made with teeth pulled from the mouths of his slaves.

Critics said selling a souvenir magnet depicting Washington's famous false teeth trivialized the fact that Washington's slaves had to give up their own teeth.

The old story that Washington's dentures were made of wood has long been known to be false. It has been known for years that Washington paid about six pounds for nine teeth that were pulled from slaves' mouths. The payment is recorded in a 1784 ledger.

Mount Vernon on its website notes that while the slaves received payment, it does not change the fact that they essentially had no choice in giving up their teeth. Mount Vernon also says that selling teeth and hair was common in the 18th century.

By The Associated Press February 19, 2020

3: Top Prices Paid For Banksy At Auction

A new day, a new record price for a Banksy artwork it seems. Show Me The Monet become the second most expensive Banksy painting ever sold at auction, selling for £7,551,60 in the Sotheby's Post Contemporary Evening Auction.

"This record price for Show me the Monet solidifies the incredible year that the Banksy market has enjoyed. Banksy has proven to be one of the most resilient assets with prices up 83% since the beginning of the year.

We're experiencing unprecedented demand from our investors in 2020 with new and growing interest internationally, but especially from the Asian market."

Top Prices Paid for Banksy at Auction:
Devolved Parliament, £9.9 million
Show Me The Monet, £7.55 million
Forgive Us Our Trespassing, £6.3 million
Mediterranean Sea View 2017, £2.23 million
Monkey Poison, £1.6 million
Keep it Spotless, £1.3 million
Vote To Love, £1,155,000
Love is in the Bin, £1.04 million
Girl with Balloon – Colour AP (Purple), £791,250
Banksy, please let's start an art feud. £731,250

By My Art Broker

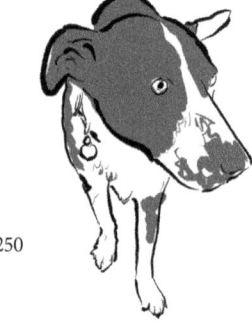

4: Walking in the Snow / Run The Jewels IV

...The way I see it you're probably freest from the ages one to four
Around the age of five you're shipped away for your body to be stored
They promise education, but really they give you tests and scores
And they predictin' prison population by who scoring the lowest
And usually the lowest scores the poorest and they look like me
And everyday on evening news they feed you fear for free
And you so numb you watch the cops choke out a man like me
And 'til my voice goes from a shriek to whisper, "I can't breathe"
And you sit there in the house on couch and watch it on TV
The most you give's a Twitter rant and call it a tragedy
But truly the travesty, you've been robbed of your empathy
Replaced it with apathy, I wish I could magically
Fast forward the future so then you can face it
And see how fucked up it'll be
I promise I'm honest, they coming for you
The day after they comin' for me
I'm readin' Chomsky, I read Bukowski
I'm layin' low for a week
I said somethin' on behalf of my people
And I popped up in Wikileaks

Thank God that I'm covered, the devil come smothered
And you know the evil don't sleep
Dick Gregory told me a couple of secrets before he laid down in his grave
All of us serve the same masters, all of us nothin' but slaves
Never forget in the story of Jesus, the hero was killed by the state....

— *Killer Mike*

5: The Popular Story of Pope Gregory IX's Great Cat Purge

The story you're most likely to find in popular history articles goes something like this:

Cats were brought to Europe from Egypt by the Romans and enjoyed a decent reputation for a long time—probably because they were such a boon to agricultural societies. Vermin did a number on harvests, but cats were nature's perfect solution: they literally can't eat anything that isn't meat, which means that they pose no risk to the crops. Meanwhile, they need that meat on the regular and know how to get it, so they're great at killing and eating vermin.

But feline-human relations deteriorated sometime in the early 1230s (CE) when Pope Gregory IX issued a papal bull called Vox in Rama. This bull, the story goes, declared cats as the instruments of Satan, and set Medieval Europe on a great cat purge, with special attention paid to black cats, who were particularly Luciferian.

So, cats went from being the targets of pagan worship to Catholic contempt for these perceived similarities to the devil. This seems to add up for the modern reader. Medieval people were indeed superstitious (but so are modern people), and cats are great but, let's face it—they're assh*les. They fly in the face of the Christian idea of God putting the natural world and its creatures here for humanity's benefit....

....

Fake Mews: The Final Word on Pope Gregory IX and Cats
..While there appears to be no evidence that Pope Gregory IX ever told people to kill cats, there have been smaller historical examples of Medieval folks killing cats for weird reasons.

Abridged Version of Alex Johnson's infamous article on Museum Hack

6: Demetri Martin's Political Correctness Joke

I wonder if robots will ever be such a regular part of our daily lives that it would be considered offensive to do the robot. You're at a party [dancing] like, "Hey man, check me out." "Whoa, what are you doing?" "Freaking robots, I don't give a shit." "Did you say 'robots? Those are Technical Americans." —*Demetri Martin, Netflix*

Thank you to all these AMAZING Models

Adriana	Benneth	Irinav	Olivia
Anastasia	Ben	Jenni	Paris
Angie	Cammie	Jesse	Pepper
Andrina	Ceasar	Katja	Sarah
Anaiv	Dan	Lola	Saju
Ayame	Dan M	Mandy	Vaunt
Baily	Edison	Moneypenny	
Becca	Elliot	Nedah	

Image Credits

The vast majority of images on pages 1-13 are with permission of Mike Woolson (https://www.jumbobrain.com/), I have made every attempt to contact and gain approval from everyone pictured. Celebrity images are included not to in any way violate publicity rights, but as an ingredient to a wholly transformative work—[They are not available for sale in isolation]. I have reached out and received permission from the people pictured (mostly from social media) as much as possible. Sharon Kihara photo by Jenny Hannah Roche. Maggie picture by Jeremy Johnson. Tami photo by Tamisaurus-Rex and #theariofthings. Star photo by Marina Bell. Rae-Leigh photo by Ana Kova Photography

The Portraits

I love drawing pictures of people. I'm fascinated by the photo you use as your profile picture. We all clearly choose something we find flattering, and they're very different, but also quite similar. I select these images from Instagram posts, Facebook profile pictures, and Mike Woolson was generous and allowed me to look through his treasure chest of party pictures. I've reached out to everyone I can to get consent. If I've missed anyone, I apologize.

It struck me how culturally significant icons and politicians are still recognizable, but in simple line, do not hold additional visual weight. The line from ordinary to gorgeous is even **more so inside** your beholding eyes. Here we're all gorgeous.

Thank you to all of you that let me include **your portrait**. I just think you're all so awesome.

cheers,

norville

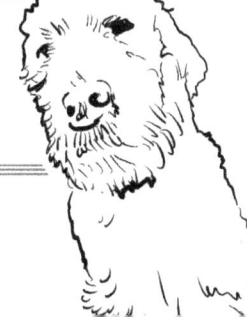

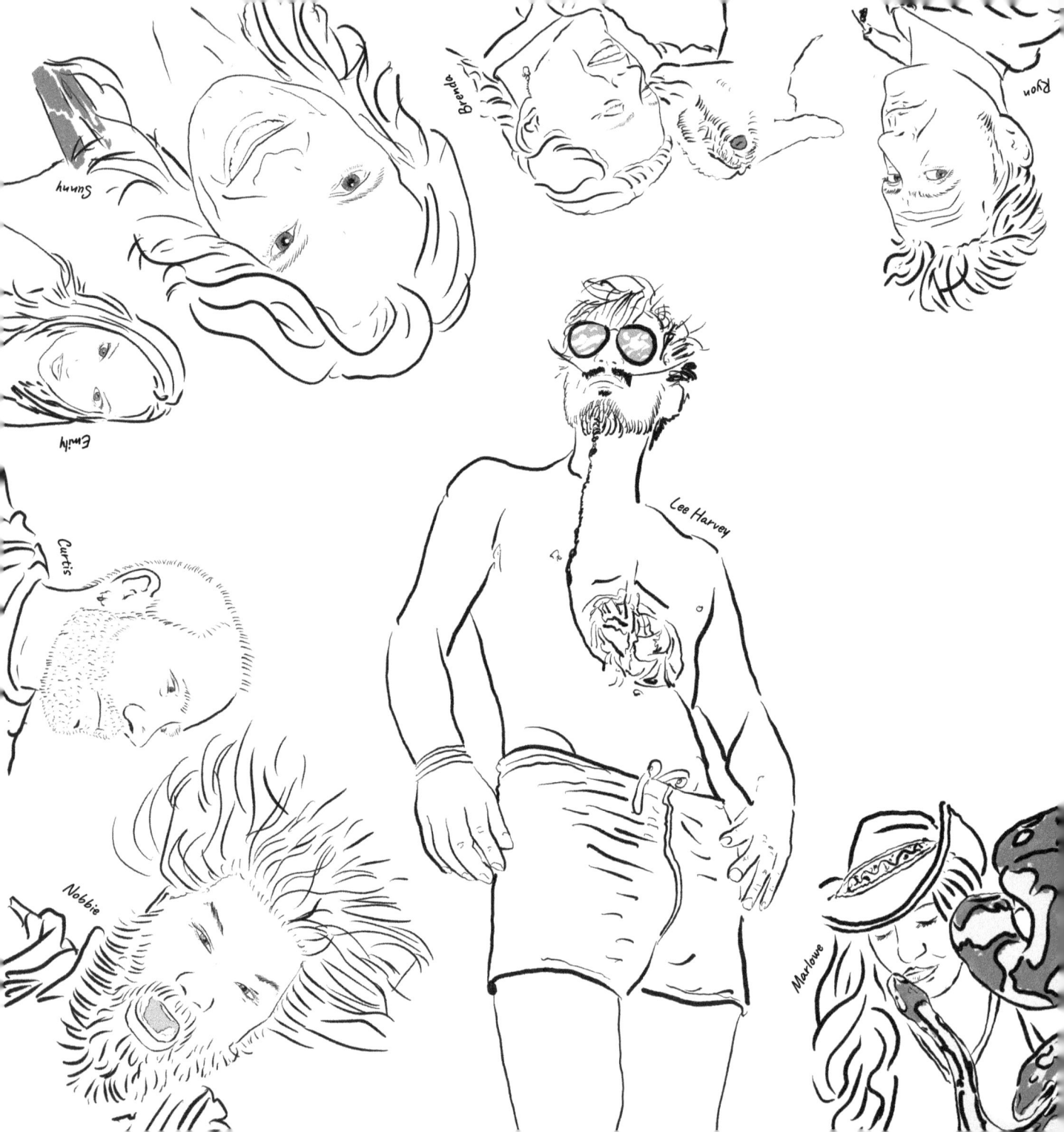

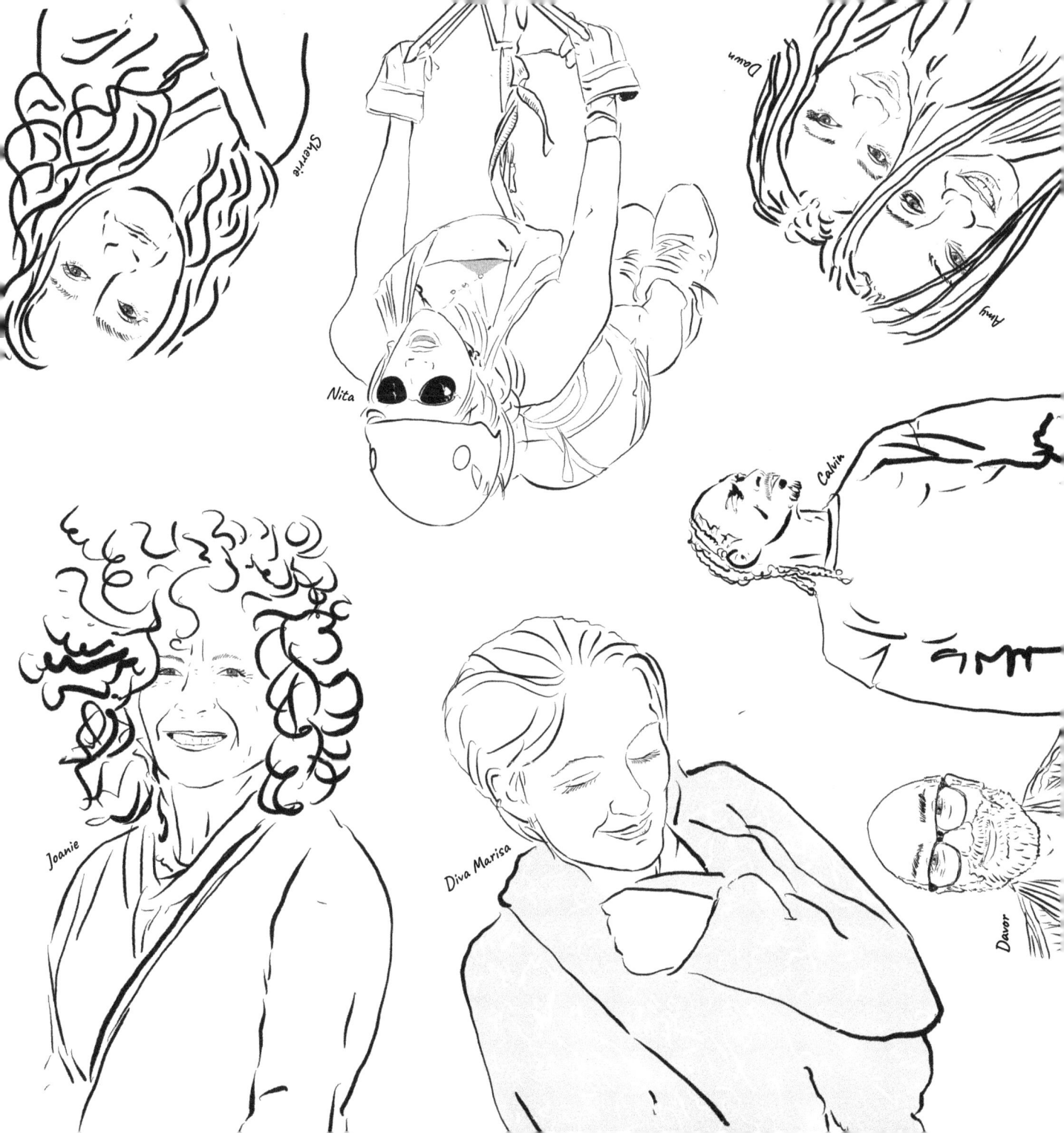

Sherrie

Nita

Dawn

Amy

Calvin

Joanie

Diva Marisa

Davor

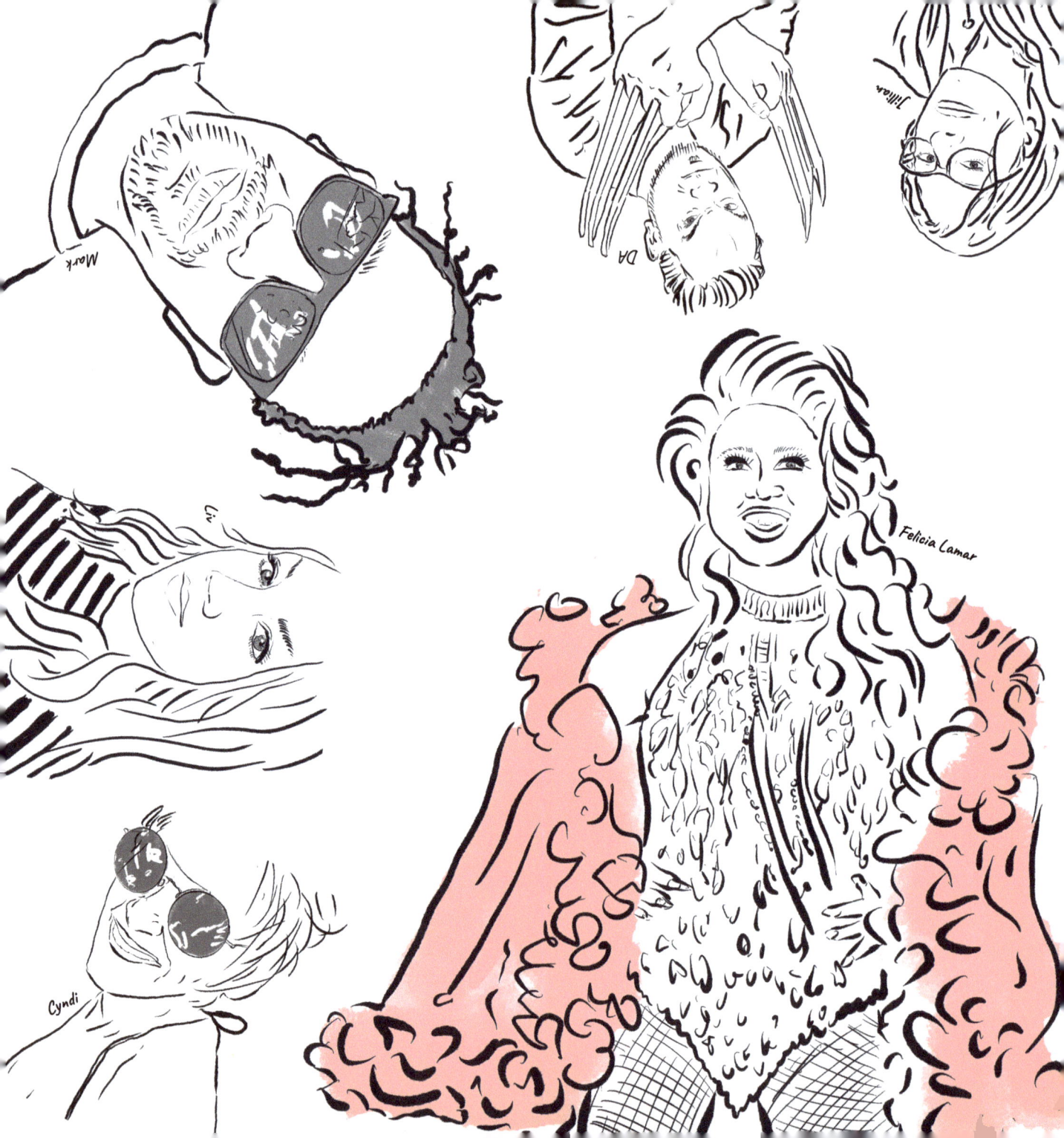

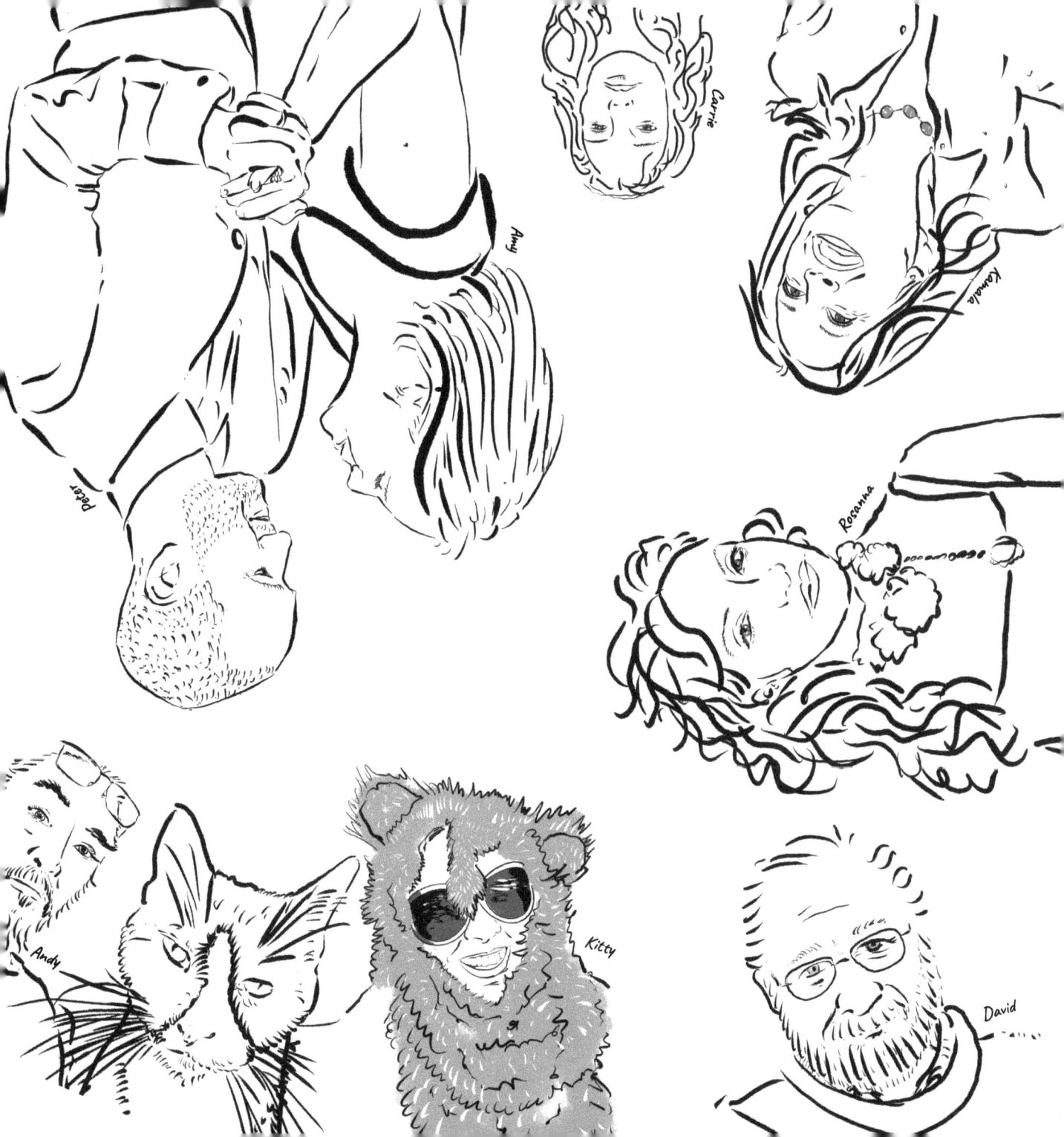

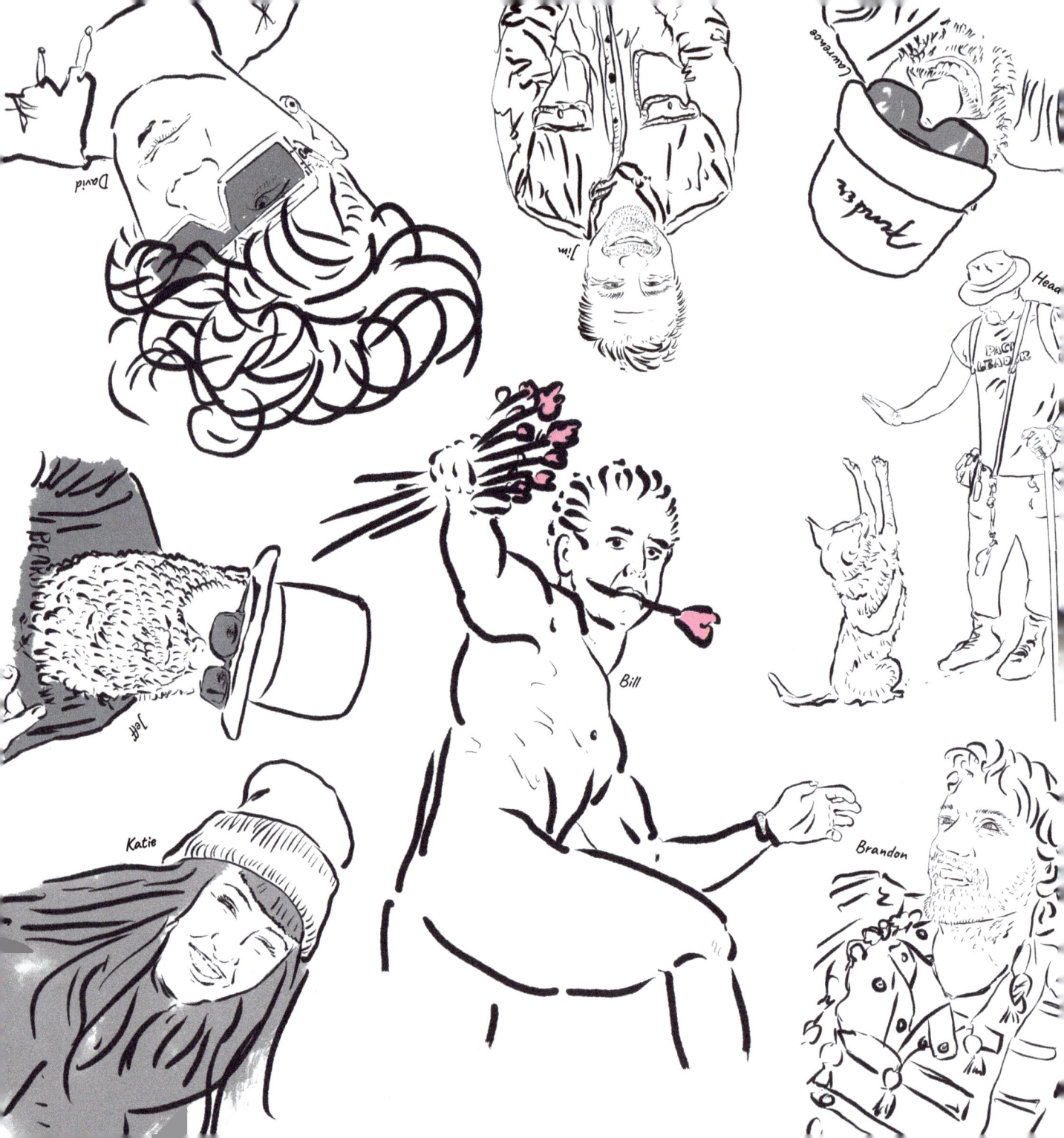

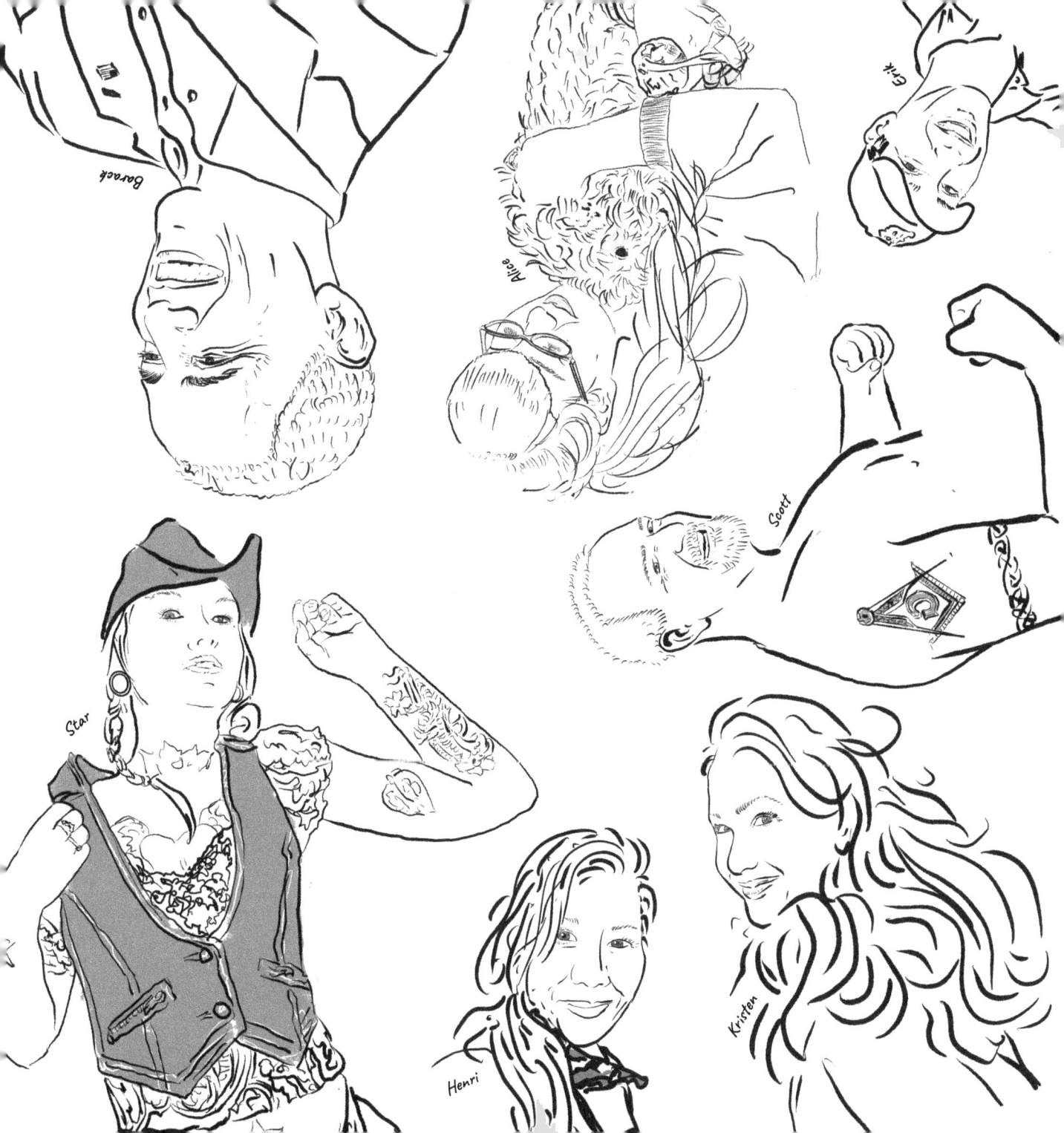

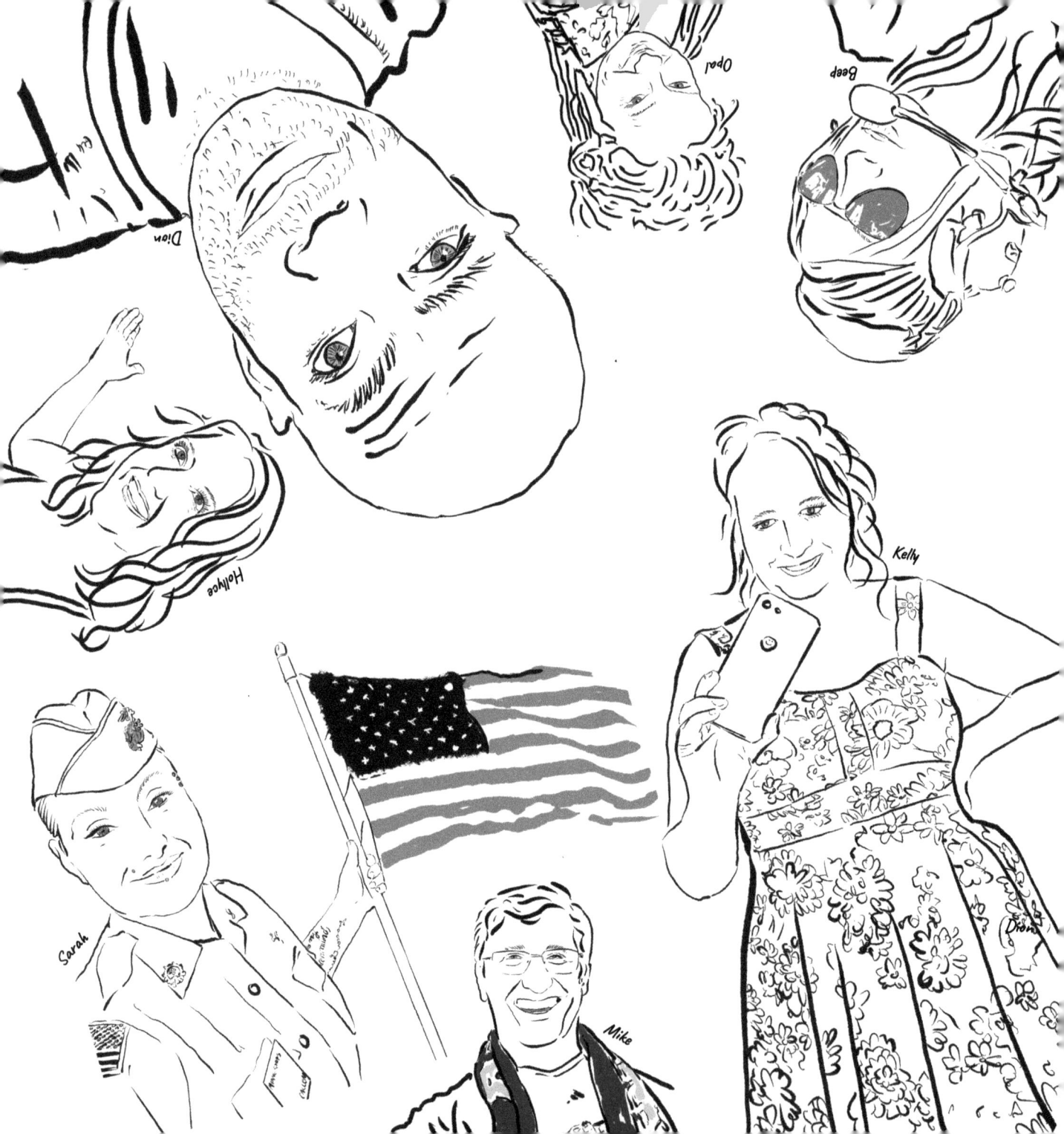

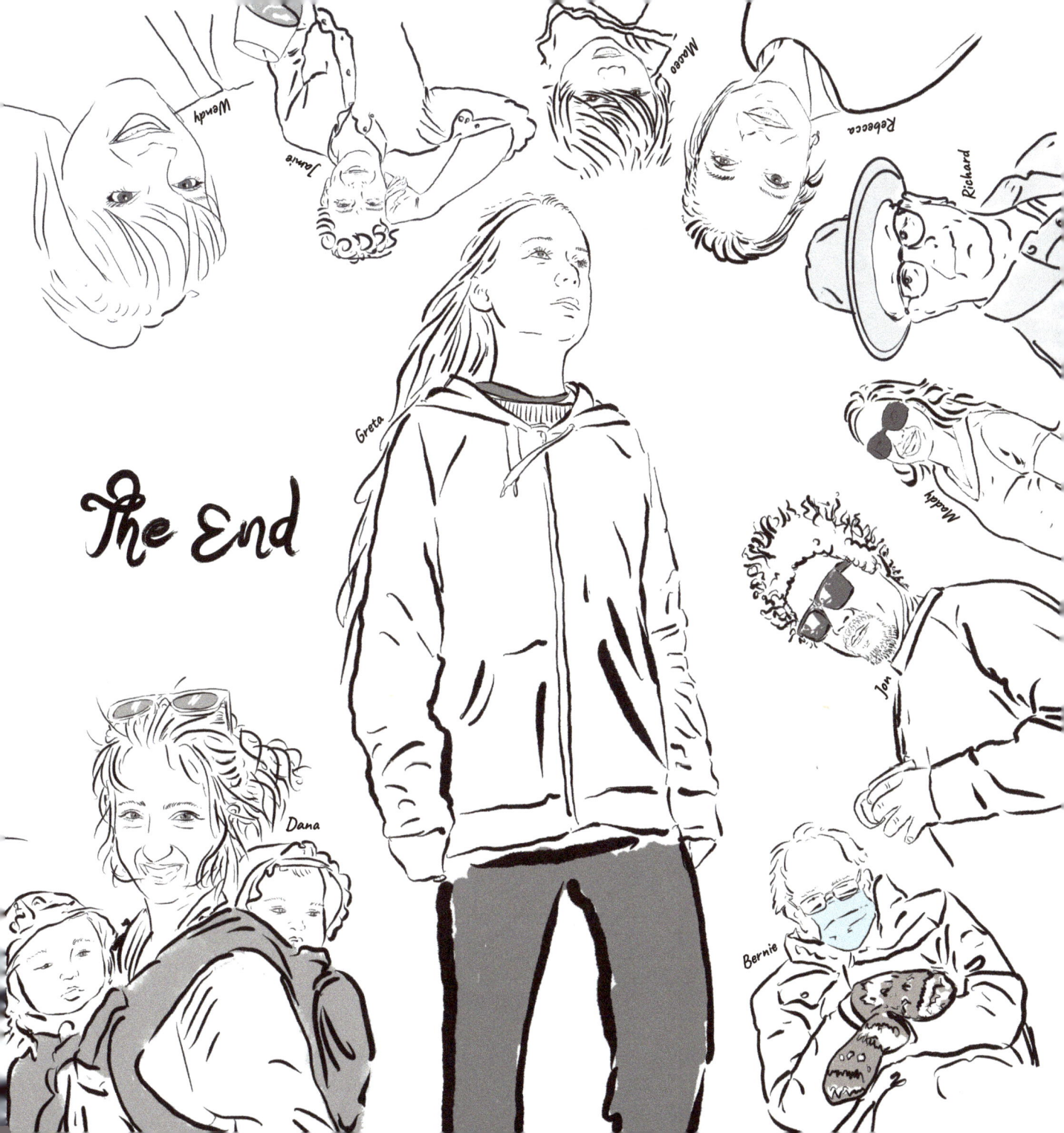

The End

Wendy
Laurie
Rebecca
Maceo
Rebecca
Richard
Greta
Maddy
Jon
Dana
Bernie

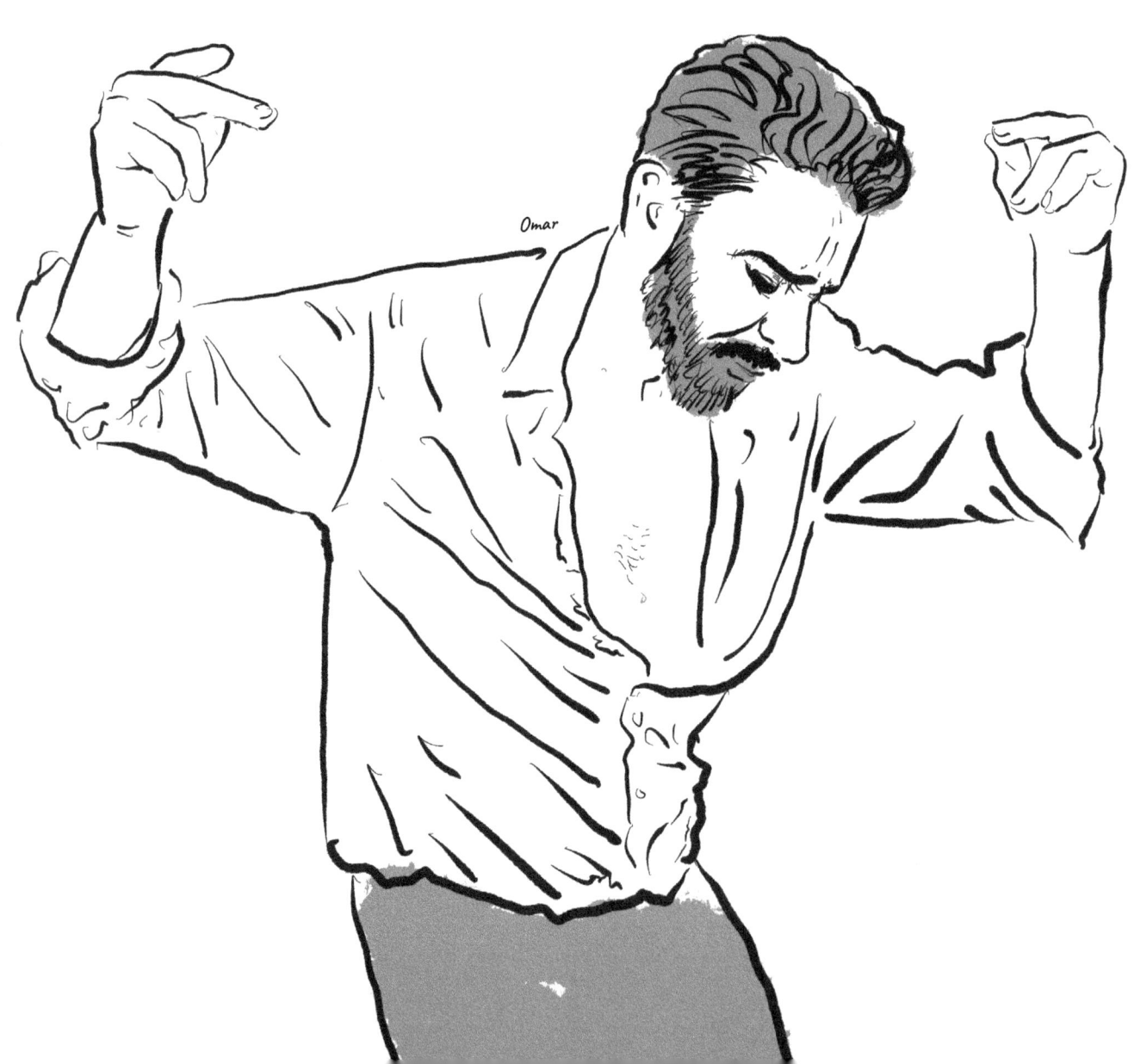

Hey Omar, the book's over.

Russ

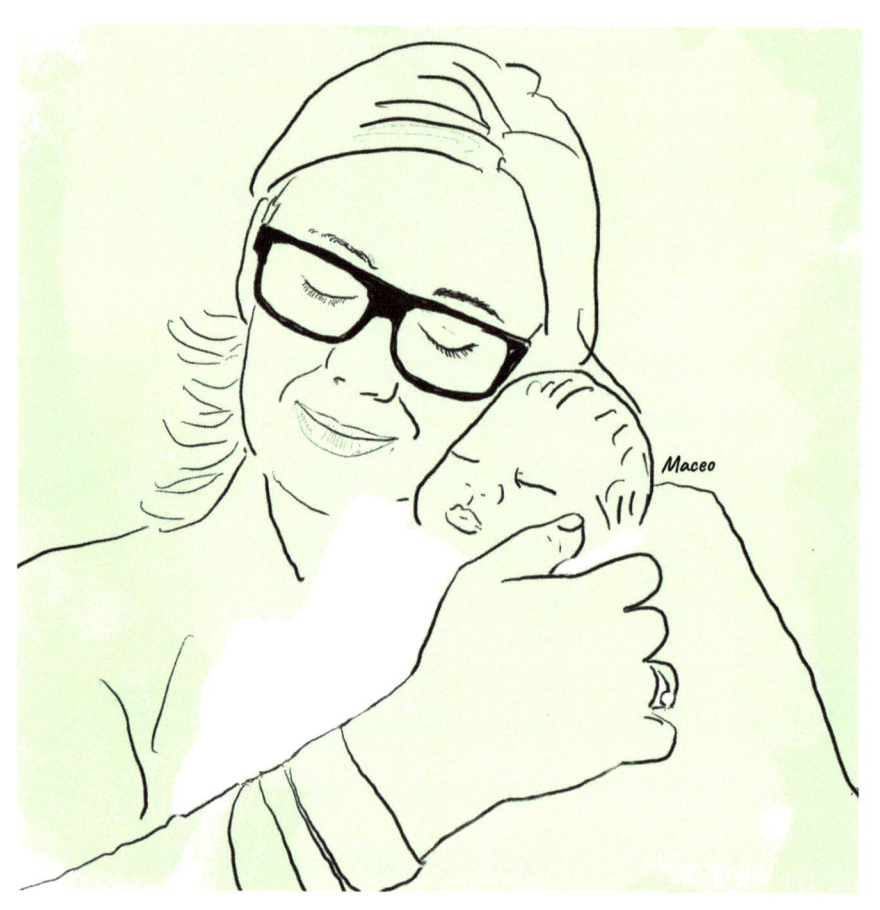

For my love Davis

CPSIA information can be obtained
at www.ICGtesting.com
Printed in the USA
BVHW020607010321
601378BV00014B/692